At the Pond

Swimming at the
Hampstead Ladies' Pond

D1381784

At the Pond

**Swimming at the
Hampstead Ladies' Pond**

DAUNT BOOKS

First published in Great Britain in 2019 by
Daunt Books
83 Marylebone High Street
London W1U 4QW

1

ISBN 978 1 911547 39 6

Typeset by Marsha Swan
Printed and bound by TJ International Ltd, Padstow, Cornwall
www.dauntbookspublishing.co.uk

Contents

CONTENTS

A Note on the Pond

The Kenwood Ladies' Pond on Hampstead Heath is one of the most magical places in London. Its sequestered location and abundant wildlife – from dragonflies, moorhens and kingfishers above the water's surface, to swan mussels, roach and carp beneath – make it a peaceful wilderness in an otherwise urban landscape.

It's also a place with a strong literary heritage. If you read closely, references to the Pond are peppered throughout novels, non-fiction and poetry. Going to the Pond can be a rite of passage; whenever you discover it, it is a place that inspires and lingers in the memory.

The ponds on Hampstead Heath are fed by natural springs originating from the River Fleet which runs subterraneously through the city. The series of ponds

known as the Highgate chain – which include the
Kenwood Ladies' Pond and the Highgate Men's Pond –
were established in the late seventeenth century as freshwater reservoirs by the Hampstead Water Company.
The Ladies' Pond was officially opened to the public for
swimming in 1925, though it is reported to have been
used unofficially for bathing long before that.

Winter

Cold Shocks and Mud Beards

ESTHER FREUD

Aged sixteen, and newly moved to London, I had no idea that Hampstead Heath existed – it was nightclubs, theatres, the smoking carriages on the tube that most excited me – but all the same I couldn't pretend to be unmoved by such a tract of nature. The trees, hills and wildflowers were so much more luxurious than the neat fields and golf courses of East Sussex, and then, to discover, hidden down a leafy lane, behind a scrub of saplings, a secluded lake for the use of women only. *No men, children, radios, dogs* – the sign on the gate warned, and as I walked down the path beside the sloping meadow, and stood on the wooden deck above the

3

mud brown pond, I had the unusual sense that I was exquisitely lucky to be female.

There are numerous ponds on Hampstead Heath, as many as thirty, but only three are reserved for swimming – a mixed, a men's and the Kenwood Ladies' Pond, which was officially opened in 1925, although women had been using it for centuries. There used to be night swimming by candlelight (now people make use of the dark to climb over the fence), and Katharine Hepburn once visited and brought a tin of biscuits for the lifeguards to have with their tea. Today there is a group of year-round swimmers who come daily, through hail or frost and dip themselves into the water. There are long winter months when it is only them. And then, at the height of summer, as many as two thousand women, of every shape and size, all classes, all ages, from across London, across the country, even from abroad, arrive to swim and sunbathe on the meadow. And the meadow is as important as the pond itself. It is a magical place, entirely private – topless sunbathing has been allowed since 1976 – and once you lie back on your towel all you can see are trees and sky. There is so much space here. So much peace. And above the birdsong the only sound is the hum of chat and laughter and the occasional scream of someone new braving the cold. You can lie in this meadow until dusk, because you've paid your dues, you've already immersed yourself in the deep, dark lake, and for now at least you don't have to go in again.

For many years I was a fair-weather swimmer, circling the pond just once on the sunniest of days, congratulating myself as I climbed out. But then, one autumn, after a difficult summer, when increasingly, a swim was the only thing that raised my spirits, I decided to keep going. I arrived, fragile and fearful, on a cold, damp Sunday morning, early, to meet a friend who'd swum through the previous year, and ignoring the temperature scrawled on the board (14°C) I took courage and followed her down the ladder. *It's so cold!* My body screamed as I struck out for the far end, anxious thoughts pursuing me, self-pity and resentment dogging my every stroke. *Why am I even doing this? What if I have a heart attack and die?* Two ducks glided by, and a heron, wise and faintly disapproving, watched me from the bank. I dipped my head under, and just like that, the mud silk of the water soothed me, released me, and when I burst up, I felt, for a moment, happy.

The next Sunday was already easier. It was a bright, crisp day and cheered by my courage in returning, I swam round twice and when I came out my body was blazing. I stood in the sunshine and chatted excitably, no need even for a towel, but within ten minutes I began to shake. The cold was like a burn: it had bedded so deep inside me I wasn't sure I'd have the strength to drag my clothes on, heave my arms into my coat. Speechless, I found my way back to the car, drove the mercifully short distance home and stood in the shower until I was warm. Later I confided in my swimming friend, and she told me I should have asked for a hug. Body heat is the best cure for hypothermia. And she advised me to invest in neoprene gloves and socks. The following week we met on the other side of the Heath and walked fast before we swam. Already warm, it was easier to get in, and harder to get out, and afterwards, although I was still shockingly cold, I arrived home tingling and ravenous, for food, for fun.

By mid-October half the pond was cordoned off. The lifeguards issued warnings. *This is proper winter swimming now. You need to come twice a week at least to acclimatise to the temperature as it plummets. Don't stay in too long. Enjoy. And don't forget to breathe.* By now most of the women were wearing bobble hats, fluorescent pink and yellow, the better to be seen in the early morning murk. But I resisted, savouring the shock of bliss as I cleared my head with a dip under the water. It released my worries. Put me in the moment. And the moment, just for a moment, was good.

On the winter equinox there was a party. Breakfast was provided, croissants, berries and tea, and the pond was hung with lanterns. As many as fifty women climbed down the ladders, struck out across the silvery lake as the sun rose above the trees. By now I was familiar with the changing room regulars – mothers who managed a quick dip after dropping off their children, women on their way to work, octogenarians who revolved in their own circle. 'See you tomorrow,' they waved merrily as they bundled off into their day. I loved being surrounded by so many women, all naked, all happy to be so as they jostled for space. It was ridiculous and oddly sexy. And a whole new etiquette had to be mastered in order to greet an acquaintance wearing only a neoprene sock.

That winter, on holiday on the Suffolk coast, I joined the Christmas Day swim. For years I'd marvelled at the insanity of anyone prepared to strip off in public in December, but this year I threw myself into the waves. By the time I came out I'd been swept so far from my starting point by the current, I had to search, my skin scorched red, through the crowd to find my clothes. But nothing mattered. I was insulated. Deep inside.

And then, in the New Year, it snowed. *Now what?* I texted. *Surely we can stay in bed today?* But I was a year-round swimmer and there was no backing down. The pond was almost entirely frozen over. There was one narrow lane where the lifeguards had broken up the ice with an oar, and there were three bobble-hatted women doing lengths. I climbed down the ladder and felt the cold cut up between my legs. It flayed my arms, cracked my skull. 'I feel good,' I used my breath to sing a snatch of James Brown, and as I plunged under I felt the water bubble round me, as refreshing as champagne.

Swimming in cold water, I read afterwards in an article pinned to the changing room wall, *raises your white blood cell count and your libido. The best way to get warm is to put your wrists in hot water.* I'd come to love this changing room. A small fuggy outhouse with one hot shower and a tap, several plastic basins, rubber mats and wall hooks, it was due to be dismantled during my first winter to make room for a larger, smarter version, and while the work was being carried out the Ladies' Pond was to close. Here was my chance to stop my swimming challenge and restart in the spring (I'd got to February after all) but the Ladies' Pond was re-allocated to the Mixed Pond, and on the weekends we were given access to the Men's. I'd never thought much of the other ponds. I was utterly loyal to my own, and had taken a condescending approach. *You've no idea*, I'd often thought as I walked past. But I found myself delighted by the leafy safety of the Mixed, and the wide expanse of the Men's, with no changing room or shower, was Spartan and surprisingly jolly. 'Everything today will be easier after this,' I said one particularly bracing morning. And a man waiting by the diving board grinned. 'Everything in life.'

In early May, the Ladies' Pond re-opened and we all
flooded back. The changing room had a slick, Swedish
feel and although there was some disgruntlement (was
this building designed by a man?), the beloved ingre-
dients remained. There was still, mostly, only one hot
shower, and there were the familiar plastic basins which
women used to splash themselves, or stood in to thaw
their feet. There was an opening party, with croissants
and berries, and when we swam the water was still
cold from the icy months before. But soon the rewards
began. From two degrees to three. From seven to eight,
up to ten. Then twelve and when it reached fourteen
it seemed so warm I was surprised I'd even shivered.
One day the temperature reached twenty-three, and
by midsummer I was positively looking forward to the
cold shocks of my second winter, the release of adren-
aline, the warmth of the deepened friendships, because
to swim in the Ladies' Pond at any time of year is
like being part of an exclusive club. There is a special
bond between the women – they smile at each other
as they glide by, and introduce their daughters to the
lifeguards as they come of age. Girls have to be eight
to swim, and when they arrive they are watched over
as they take their first strokes. Now, each time I walk
down the shaded path I think of the friends I've swum
with over thirty years, the new friends I've made more
recently. When we meet we laugh and congratulate

ourselves and remind each other to wipe the mud beards off our chins. And we need to be reminded because when you rise up out of the velvety water you feel so powerfully beautiful that it's possible to forget to look into a mirror for the rest of the day.

It's well known that swimming in cold water has physical benefits but there are others that are harder to define. Swimming past waterlilies and nesting ducks, breathing in the watermelon scent of the mud, sailing in slow breaststroke past weeping willows. It is all so different from the pounding lengths of a traditional pool where it is possible to drag your worries with you from one end to the other. Here, my sense of myself was altered, the cold too shocking to focus on sorrow and confusion when the useful thing was courage, and when my heart had steadied, and I realised I was not actually going to die, the exhilaration hit me and I felt dizzyingly grateful to be alive.

Winter Swimming

LOU STOPPARD

Winter season at the Kenwood Ladies' Pond on Hampstead Heath begins when the water temperature drops below twelve degrees, usually around mid-September. Then, a rope is attached to buoys to limit the distance swimmers can go – it creates a neat arc to lap, dissecting the 100m by 50m pond. You look wistfully at the rest, remembering a time when things were warm.

The water is silky. It's thicker than other water. It sticks to the skin, laps your body and holds you, suspended. You cut through it, as if stirring cream. It's nearly black, you can barely make out your limbs, and sometimes as you peel off your wet costume there are mud stains on your flesh, but you always feel cleaner when you get out than before you got in. A shower feels like a shame – that would just be normal water.

When the temperature is just a couple of degrees, your feet and hands stiffen, and you wonder if someone could actually cut into your flesh without you noticing such is the anesthetising effect, but somehow the water still feels gentle. You emerge, skin red, endorphins boisterous, and wonder why all of London isn't here, at 8 a.m. on an icy day, bidding good morning to the ducks.

A small chalk board outside the lifeguards' station advertises the temperature: six degrees in November, maybe three or four in December, a noteworthy one in January. A good rule for winter swimming is to never stay in for more minutes than the number of degrees. When it falls to almost zero, you lower yourself in, wincing, from one metal ladder and hurtle towards the other, a mere few metres away. It's more of a dip than a swim. Dithering on the ladder is impossible; the cold will get to you. You have to speed in, throw yourself forward, ready for the shock.

But what do you wear? Surely a wetsuit, people ask. No, just a bathing suit, I reply, choreographing nonchalance. Before, I wore small neoprene socks. That was three years ago, when I first began visiting the Heath. I swam there initially simply to see if I could overcome the fear of the inky depth. I'd started to notice a flutter of alarm when in deep water, and thought maybe this would kick me out of it. I went back each week, refusing to break the routine largely due to stubbornness – once September had become October and then November, the thought of giving up felt like accepting some defeat. Now my body has acclimatised. It has adapted to tolerate the cold, to mute that feeling of a thousand stabbing pins, and I go barefoot. I am truly a winter swimmer.

'Women Only,' reads the sign at the gate, 'Men not allowed beyond this point.' It's hardly inviting. 'This water is deep and cold. Competent swimmers only.' A long path takes you from the gate to the water. You can do it in 150 steps, directed by a canopy of trees. On a Tuesday morning in December, a lone swimmer is far away near the limit rope, as far out as she's allowed. Closer, three women gasp as they try to overcome the bite. The coldest part is the ground right before the water, unkind concrete on naked soles. The water is fantastic for anxiety – when you swim in such low temperatures, your brain is lurched out of any spiralling, forced to only focus on the cold. It's a welcome distraction from the imagined horrors beneath, the north London ghouls and Hampstead great whites that could be moving in the metres of dark, ever so close to brushing your feet. You will your lungs to steady themselves, to take in air calmly. You force your legs to move. You spread your fingers wide, hands arched like a nervous spider, trying to keep any feeling alive. Movement is the only way to keep going – and the only way out.

There are 1,348 names on the winter swimming register kept at the Ladies' Pond. According to Nicky Mayhew, co-chair of the Kenwood Ladies' Pond Association, a voluntary organisation of 'women who care about the pond', this is far more than they had ten years ago and reflects the current enthusiasm for 'wild' swimming. The association estimates that there are about 150 women who actually swim regularly through the winter.

The pond women are alert and witchy. You find them half naked, clutching quick-dry towels and fuzzy bobble hats, which they keep on while swimming to avoid losing body heat. They are mostly older women: a gaggle of different bodies, curves and rolls and wise wrinkles. 'My first swim in the Pond was about 1960,' says Anne Burley, who is eighty-two. 'I didn't swim regularly until about 1972. And I've been swimming every day since 1980, give or take a year I spent in Croatia, working for the UN.' Each day, she walks twenty minutes from her home in Highgate to the water's edge. Others come from Bloomsbury, Stoke Newington or Camden – one cycles from Battersea every day, ready for the Pond to open, as it does all year round, at 7 a.m. Burley never decisively committed herself to swimming through the winter – 'I just thought, I'll go on for a bit longer. Then by the time it gets really, really cold, your body gets used to it. It's so much a habit with me now. It's what I do. I wake up in the morning and I go and swim.' She favours a gentle breaststroke. A pool doesn't compare. 'It's just so boring. You go up and down. Whereas the Pond, you go in different directions, and around, and you can look at things while you're swimming. It's wonderful to have all this nature around – and, of course, the possibility of seeing the kingfisher.'

When Burley began winter swimming there were just a handful of women willing to bear the cold and no hot showers. There were only two lifeguards, who did alternate shifts – 'If they were in a good mood they would bring you a little bucket of hot water, which they had to boil up. And we'd all take our turn at dipping our feet in it.' Today, a small wooden hut that looks almost Scandinavian contains a handful of private changing rooms and four showers – two hot, two cold. There are always a few lifeguards on duty now. They nod as you approach the water – 'Are you OK with the temperature? Have you swum here before?'

In and out of the water, the pond women talk of their children, their work, their marriages, their divorces

– life, and, of course, the cold. Burley recalls women supporting each other through strokes, falls, floods and double mastectomies. 'You get a bit resentful in the summer when the Pond is crowded with "other" people but we try and repress these unworthy instincts and be more welcoming.'

In the summer, the Pond becomes something of a social hub. A flock of younger swimmers descend. Every spot on the greens that surround the water is taken up by women chatting and arguing and reading and sunbathing and people-watching. If men could see this they would correctly call it paradise. Is this what they imagine women do when they hang out together: sit topless, hair dripping, smoking a cigarette, reading the newspaper, eating leftovers from a Tupperware, momentarily unbothered by stares or comments.

When it's hot, the Pond recalls the early optimism of John Cheever's short story 'The Swimmer' before darkness descends, when the drinks are plentiful, the mood still light and the water like a bath – 'The day was beautiful and it seemed to him that a long swim might enlarge and celebrate its beauty.' A swim in the Pond is a prelude to sensual summer affairs: walking through the city as the light fades, and long nights at the pub drinking outside until you can't drink any more. In the winter, it's something more serious. The aims are less social, more of a personal quest – a search for stillness, escape, a desire to overcome something, a need to prove one *can*. Winter swimmers are there to be alone, together.

To swim is to enter a new state. You go 'through the looking glass', says Roger Deakin, the late British nature-lover, who, in *Waterlog*, details his quest to swim across Britain, through lakes, moats, pools, ponds and rivers. He likens entering the water to being born, moving rapidly from one norm to another. Suddenly, the process has been reversed and you are back in the womb, floating. 'In water, all possibilities seem infinitely extended.' You are, he writes, 'free of the tyranny of gravity and the weight of the atmosphere.' In the Pond, your body moves differently – legs punch around and scoop, arms kick. D. H. Lawrence understood. Many of his characters share a yearning to be transformed by water. In *The White Peacock* he describes two friends leaping into a pond and mustering the strength to move, to *swim*. 'The water was icily cold, and for a moment deprived me of my senses. When I began to swim, soon the water was buoyant. And I was sensible of nothing but the vigorous poetry of action.' To swim is to meditate – that's what he's saying.

Julia Dick started swimming in her early fifties, finding the Pond a welcome escape from a draining career as a lawyer. She is now sixty-three and the co-chair of the Ladies' Pond Association. She is the sports teacher you deserved – darting eyes and toothy smile and a tuneful, encouraging voice. 'The sense of equilibrium you get from it is partly to do with being supported in the water. You're actually brought back to your barest self – the one that can meet the world, and that is supported by nature. Being held by the water, is, for me, an amazing thing,' she says. She swims every other day. 'I put on my swimming costume and I walk across the Heath. The idea that you would come home without going swimming is just preposterous. It's never the same, but it's always beautiful. It's a welcoming space, it recognises the struggle, the daily struggle, the discrimination many women face in life. The Pond can support you through crises. It helped me with the death of my parents. And with menopause, all the mood changes.'

'That pond holds a lot of tears,' says fifty-three-year-old Toby Brothers, who runs literary salons. When she talks about the Pond, her eyes widen with each adjective. She calls the approach, 'a perfect green grotto'. To her, it's all a miracle. 'There is something about being in really cold water where you do strip off the shields that we build. You make yourself more vulnerable and so then being able to talk about things that are close or hard is easy. And you have to move back into your body again, in a really significant way.' The blood rushes to your organs, and you feel revived. You feel powerful, regal. If you can hurl yourself into a freezing pond, you can likely do anything, you think. Brothers has swum every winter for ten years. 'The first year was hard, but I did it. And I still can't believe I did it. I still can't believe I *do* it.'

The more regularly you swim, the more the pond ladies come to recognise you. They offer approving nods when you emerge, wet. They provide titbits of advice. 'I love the older women there,' says Brothers. 'That's partly why I do it. Our culture deals so badly with ageing and the pond community is full of these shining older women.' She recalls them regaling her with the benefits of pond swimming, on how you come to feel your body so much more. 'They are so funny – one of them said to me in my first year, "It makes sex better".'

In the winter, the Pond seems wilder. The trees sag and shake, depositing snow drops, the reeds ripple and the wind circles above. European friends cannot understand the appeal. The *cold*, they say, grimacing. New Yorkers are even more confused. There, the outdoor pools close in early September, when the weather is still balmy. Are there eels? Fish? they ask. Yes, you reply. So, it's really just a pond, they say, keen for evidence of a bottom, or barriers, or concrete sides or something more reassuringly manmade.

Sometimes, the water is covered in ice. In the past, if it was entirely frozen, the lifeguards would crack it open, making a small gap for swimmers. Now, that is avoided. If the Ladies' Pond is iced over, women are welcome to take a trip down the hill to the Men's Pond in search of moving water – a rare moment of access. A real treat is when it sleets or rains – and the droplets splash into the water from up high and the view becomes blurred and dreamy. The surrounding branches and grasses become your conspirators. You are the 'emancipated mole' from *The Wind in the Willows*, who has finally embraced the freedom offered by water – 'with his ear to the reed-stems he caught, at intervals, something of what the wind went whispering so constantly among them'.

And then, one day, twelve degrees comes and the line rope will be taken away, and you can make your way to the end of the Pond for the first time, again. You know summer is starting, with all the promise that brings. Until then, the cold is still there to be overcome.

So, each week, I split into the deep. The ladder gets smaller and smaller as I close in on the line limit, and, as always, I eventually catch my breath.

Pond: A Dendrochronology

JESSICA J. LEE

Unremitting, the same rain that had fallen for the entire week poured from the rooftop. It dripped over the corners of the old green shelter, down the concrete jetty, patterning the pond with pinpricks. Wet already, I slipped into the black and swam a small loop, my breath catching on the sharp edges of the cold.

I'd been swimming most days that winter, lowering myself into the pond despite a banged-up shoulder and a gripping depression. Work had called me there, into the water, like some small miracle: I was writing a doctoral dissertation about the Heath and exploring ideas of beauty and history with the Pond's winter swimmers. I spent my days swimming and interviewing between bouts of intense research in archives across London and as far away as Scotland.

That day at the Pond in mid-February, I was alone but for the lifeguards. After I climbed out, towelled the shimmer of ice off my skin and returned to my clothes, I sat on the bench beneath the awning, sipping from a thermos of stale but hot tea. A duck and a cormorant toddled beneath the shelter, too. Jane, one of the lifeguards who taught me to swim in winter, stood in front of me, not guarding the Pond but in her civilian gear, working a hand-shave across a slice of ringed and mottled oak. A small, gnarled pile of sawdust grew in the wake of her movements.

The tree had been felled in the days before – part of the clearance works that would precede the demolition of the very spot on which I sat, the old green hut from the seventies and the small shelter of its awning. Workers began digging to rebuild the dams that ran between ponds. The trees that came down were mostly put to use elsewhere on the Heath, as fences and dead-hedges, but this one – a sturdy English oak that had grown on the southern edge of the pond – Jane had asked to keep.

What she planned to do with it, she didn't yet know. The trunk laid prone, split in two, in the meadow behind the hut. But this single slice, crescent-shaped, thirty-six inches across, sat shaved and smoothed on the dock. Swimmers passed by it as they ventured into the water, and then stood marvelling at its perfect rings when they were out once more.

A sturdy inch of bark blanketed its sides, the wood vermillion beneath its surface, before becoming creamy sapwood. The heartwood alternated brown and bruise-blue, until the wood's inner pith – the colour of cacao – spiralled into the timber's tight centre. The scars of a heart shake cut across its inner rings, a dark star across the first decades of the tree's life. Irregularities like heart shakes harden into wood as it grows, revealed only once a tree is felled. It grew in the interplay of heat and frost, when the wood responded to pressure, just as the water expanded and contracted with winter and thaw. The heart shake was a marker of transformation.

Dendrochronology is a method of dating trees by their rings, of matching the circular bands of a tree's growth with the steady unfurling of time, year on year. Storms, bad winters, droughts and disturbance are all rendered in the rings of a tree, in darker and in lighter tones, in thicker and thinner bands. Historical events too can be matched to the stages in a tree's growth: it is possible to see the spoils of war written into wood, bomb explosions marking scorched rings into the timeline.

The formation of rings is not unique to trees. Shells do much the same thing, forming notched ridges in their calcite growth. After the digging started, Jane gave me the gift of a shell dredged from the muck, a glossy, brittle bivalve that shone opalescent in the light. The shell had preceded the pond – a record of a time when this place was undersea – and had been unearthed with things far from its time: a scrap of clay pipeline, narrow as a drinking straw, and a piece of polished glass. I counted the rings of the shell's life, banded on its surface.

I spent those winter months of my research puzzling over the waters, in the archives learning about the clay puddling and old dams used on the Heath, and in the Pond, swimming. I studied the old spa, the iron-rich chalybeate springs that drew people to this place, pulling old paintings from the archives to search for water. The Highgate pond chain had an uncertain history: the ponds were created between the end of the seventeenth and the beginning of the eighteenth centuries, when the Hampstead Water Company leased land at Millfield to channel the streams of the Fleet. I could say with some certainty how the Heath had looked in previous centuries, where ponds once stood and where fields had grown over. I could guess at when the trees grew up.

The trees were bare boned in the dark season, so I could just about see through to the fields beyond, as the pond had looked a lifetime ago. No trees had circled the shoreline when the pond became the Pond.

But when sheep and grazing cows were moved off the Heath in the twentieth century, the scrub in all its fields grew into forest. The meadows grew long without their flocks, and the hedges grew out into woodland. Perhaps to give swimming women shelter, more trees were planted.

Brittle as a film of crystals on boiled sugar, the sheet of ice that had encased the Pond wilted with the winter rain. That delicate cold mixed with the pond water, clear and thin and black. The space of the Pond, enclosed by trees, felt vacated, quiet, distinct. When I got in the water each day, my thoughts ceased to a similar silence.

The other women had taught me a few things about winter: to count my strokes – forty-five at the minimum – and to feel the small twinges of pain and numbness that shivered through my limbs. One swimmer told me she could feel a twitch in her thumb when it was time to get out. So I listened, my mind occupied only with sensation, as I watched the light sway dappled on the water.

I had swum there for many years and knew the slick of the Pond well. The velvet of summer settled to a sharp clarity in winter. My movements stiffened in the cold, and I coursed slowly between the white rings. My legs swayed deep below the surface. Ahead of me moved a lip of water, a wave pushed by my body, silken and bowed, uncatchable. Each stroke I made chasing it was written concentric on the pond, my small waves radiating towards the shore.

The oak remained on the dock for a few days, a passing curiosity clamped to a bench. I watched the women come and count, still swim-capped and clutching towels round their wet frames, as they traced their fingernails across the wood's smoothed surface.

'This was the year I was evacuated during the Blitz,' one surmised of the heartwood.

'This was the year I first came to the Pond,' said another. She counted backwards, bark to pith, to 1978.

I crouched and counted, as they all had. Eighty-two years concentric, give or take. Summer rings and winter rings, lightened and darkened. The wide bands of good weather years, and the tightened growth of dry ones.

One of the swimmers was eighty-two that year, so the women came to associate the tree with her, growing tall and lean and sturdy by the water. We tried to guess at whether the tree was the wilding sprout of a neighbouring oak, or if it had been planted, knowing that little of this small wilderness – the pond included – was naturally occurring.

In the early 1930s, it was said King George V made a visit to the Pond. To mark the occasion, an oak had been planted. Was it ours?

This tree had grown there nonetheless, on the shore between our pond and the birds', and the women had come to know it. Not as a stand-out tree, individual like the willow, but as one of many on our ringed horizon, as part of the arboreal shelter that made the Pond feel private. Jane's hand-drawn map of the Pond's trees – posted on the notice board some years before – had shown the oak, a frilled crown of leaves and a cursive label. Without that map, without its felling, I may never have noticed it was there.

In late February, the chalkboard on the wall read three degrees. The air was much the same. Rain still fell, sending ripples into the water with the regularity of a hypnotist's spiral. The slice of oak had darkened in the damp weather, absorbing the moisture that fell from the sky to the pond. I greeted the wood, took a photograph so I could sketch it later, and then ducked into the changing room to slip out of my clothes.

The water was thickening with the rain, leaf mulch rising after days of bad weather. The once-leaves moved as I did, bobbing on the crests of the waves I made, tracing a course to the rings and back again, repeated. My heart shaking with the cold, I watched the trees as I swam, silent without their flicker of leaf, and thought that in their stillness I sensed something of movement.

Spring

Small Bodies of Water

NINA MINGYA POWLES

The swimming pool is on the edge of a hill overlooking the valley where the town begins. From up here I can almost see Mt Kinabalu's dark rainforests. I have never been there, but I know the names of things that live among the trees from looking at Gung Gung's natural history books: the Bornean sucker fish, the Kinabalu serpent eagle, the enormous *Rafflesia* flower, the Atlas moth with white eyes on its wings.

Sara and I are the same age, born a month apart, but she already knows how to dive headfirst into the deep end. I lower myself down the cold metal ladder and swim out after her, kicking up a spray of white waves behind me, until my toes dip down and there is nothing there to catch me. I reach for the edge, gasping. I am happier here where there's something solid to hold onto, where I can see our splashes making spiral patterns on the hot concrete. From here, I use my legs to push myself down. I hover here in my safe corner of the deep end, waiting to see how long I can hold my breath. Looking up through my goggles I see rainforest clouds and a watery rainbow. I see the undersides of frangipani petals floating on the surface, their gold-edged shadows moving towards me. I straighten my legs and point my toes and launch myself towards the sun.

Gung Gung used to drive us to the Sabah Golf Club pool whenever we came to visit. He went off for his morning round of golf while my cousin Sara and I went straight to the pool, my mum and her mum lagging behind us. Po Po, my grandmother, stayed behind as usual. Over many years of visiting my grandparents in Malaysia, I can never remember Po Po coming with us to the pool.

Where is the place your body is anchored? Which body of water is yours? If I looked at a map of the place where I was born, it could be easy. But I was four years old when we moved for the first time; we would move three more times after that. In his essay *Mixed-Race Superman*, Will Harris writes that the mixed-race person 'grows up to see the self as something strange and shifting . . . shaped around a lack.' Is it that I've anchored myself to too many places at once, or nowhere at all? The answer lies somewhere between. Over time, springing up from the in-between space, new shapes form. I am many mountains. I am many bodies of water, strange and shifting.

In truth, my first body of water was the swimming pool. Underwater, I was like one of the little fish with silver eyes that Gung Gung catalogued and preserved in gold liquid in jars on the shelf in the room where I slept, trapped there forever, glimmering. The pool was where I first taught myself to do an underwater somer-sault, first swam in deep water and first learned how to point my toes, hold my legs together and kick out in a way that made me feel powerful. In the pool, we spent hours pretending to be mermaids, though I thought of myself more as some kind of ungraceful water creature, since I didn't have very long hair and wasn't such a good swimmer. Perhaps half orca, half girl.

On a beach on the Kāpiti Coast of New Zealand, a place I came to know as *back home*, my mother and I wade out across the sand to where shallow waves lap against our calves. Buckets in hand, we feel with our toes for pipi shells poking up through the sand. At the place where the Waikanae estuary widens and empties into the sea, I stand at the edge of the low sandbank and push hard with the balls of my feet. Cracks form in the sand like an ice sheet breaking apart. At the slightest touch of my foot, tiny sand cliffs go crumbling beneath me into the shallow estuary. The slow current shifts to make room for the new piece of shore I've created. I learn that with the lightest pressure I am capable of causing a small rupture, a fault.

Sometimes home is a collection of things that have fallen or been left behind: dried agapanthus pods, the exoskeletons of cicadas (tiny ghosts still clinging to the trees), the discarded shells of quail's eggs on Po Po's plate, cherry pips in the grass, the drowned chrysanthemum bud in the bottom of the teapot. Some things are harder to hold in my arms: the smell of salt and sunscreen, mint-green blooms of lichen on rock, wind-bent pōhutukawa trees, valleys of driftwood.

When I got my first period when I was eleven, it was swimming that I was most afraid of. Not of attracting sharks in shallow waters like boys stupidly said we might, as if they could somehow scare us more than our own bodies already had. I had visions of trailing blood around the swimming pool, not knowing it was coming from me. I had no concept yet of what my body could contain; I thought I might stain everything red in my wake. In English class we watched *The Diary of Anne Frank*, the black-and-white film version. In one scene, there was a small pool of blood seeping into the middle of Anne's bedsheets and some boys looked away.

There were pink crabs scuttling along the bottom of the outdoor pool next to my international school in the outskirts of Shanghai. They shone through the chlorine like bright, fleshy gems. We were shocked to see the tiny creatures here, right under our feet, in this colourless stretch of land where there were no birds or insects apart from mosquitoes. The sea was a dark mass just beyond the golf course and a concrete sea wall. It was always there but its presence felt remote. I felt an urge to scoop up the crabs in my hands and carry them back over the wall that separated us from the biggest body of water I had ever known, the Yangtze River Delta, and beyond that, the East China Sea.

In the concrete city of Shanghai, the over-chlorin-
ated pool became our sanctuary. It sparkled aquama-
rine against a skyline of dust. Underwater everything
was different, bathed in holy silence and blue echoes.
The slanted windows cast wavering lines of liquid
light beneath the surface. We felt the way our bodies
moved, lithe and strong and new. We pushed off from
the edge into the blue again and again, diving deeper
and deeper each time.

When we moved back to Wellington I taught myself
not to be afraid of open water. There was no sand, only
pebbles and driftwood and shells. Everything scraped
against us, left a mark on our skin: rocks, wind, salt.
The cold hurt initially but we pushed ourselves headfirst into the waves and came up screaming, laughing.
I pushed away my thoughts of jellyfish and stingrays,
the ones the orca sometimes come to hunt. The shore
in sight, I floated on my back and let the ocean hold
me in its arms. Big invisible currents surged up from
beneath, rocking me closer. I dipped my head backwards to find tiny Mākaro Island hanging upside down
in my vision, perfectly symmetrical and green, as if it
had only just risen out of the sea.

The harbour carried debris from a summer storm just passed – shattered driftwood, seaweed blooms, plastic milk-bottle caps, the occasional earlobe jellyfish. The further out I swam, I found a layer of clear, molten blue. My friend Kerry and I dove above and below the rolling waves. At this moment in our lives neither of us was sure where home was exactly, but underwater, the question didn't seem to matter. Emerging from nowhere a black shape drew close to my body and I lurched, reaching for Kerry, but then I saw the outline of wings. Kawau pū, the native New Zealand black cormorant, or shag as it's often known. It was mid-dive, eyes open, wings outstretched and soaring down into the deep. Another wave rises over us and we turn our bodies towards it, opening.

I was in my small bedroom in Shanghai on 13 November 2016, when the words 'magnitude 7.8' appeared at the top of my Twitter feed, followed by a tsunami evacuation warning for all coastal areas in central New Zealand. I sent messages to my parents and refreshed the page over and over while imagining the tide dropping away in the dark. They piled the dog into the back of the car and drove a short way up the hill, listening to the unsettled night. The warning was lifted two hours later, but the islands kept shifting. A long way south, four-metre waves came unseen in the night, pushing kelp and crabs up onto the land but harming no one. In some places along the coast of Kaikoura, the seabed lifted up by two metres. The words I heard broadcast on the Radio NZ livestream chimed inside my head for days. *Do not go anywhere near water. The first wave may not be the largest.*

Almost two years later, on another continent, I was near a body of water when I received a phone call from my mother to say Po Po had died. She had caught pneumonia in the night and her small lungs could not cope. The River Thames flowed darkly beneath me, carrying pieces of the city out to sea. I stared down at the current and used the rhythm of its flow to regulate my breathing.

The Ladies' Pond is hidden in a meadow in a corner of Hampstead Heath. I go alone to find it one day during an April heatwave. I put my green swimsuit on under my clothes and pack my purple backpack: a towel, water, two peaches and a Kit Kat. I pass the sign at the gate that says 'Men not allowed beyond this point' and head down the gravel track towards the trees. I notice that the wooden bench where I've left my things is engraved with the phrase 'RECLAIM THE NIGHT', and I suddenly feel like I have reached a place that is a sacred part of many women's lives. Now it's a part of mine, too. Here, it is safe and wondrous for me to be alone. The sunlit pond is fringed with reeds and willows and tiny blue dragonflies skim about the surface. Lowering myself down from the platform at the edge, I launch myself into the water too quickly. The cold shocks my skin, shoves air out from my lungs. I take deep breaths with my lips close together, trying to steady my heart.

I didn't know Po Po well; I can't speak Hakka, the language of my mum's side of the family, and she spoke little English. Our shared language was food. When we got back from the pool she brought out plates of sticky fried chicken, aubergine and coconut curry, fried bananas wrapped in paper. She watched us from the head of the table, her eyes sparkling. A few years ago I gave her a copy of my first poetry book. She smiled and mouthed the title slowly, tasting the letters, her voice catching on the edges of these English words she knows but hasn't often said aloud. '*Drift*,' she said, 'What is *drift*?'

Longing to be closer to the Pond, my boyfriend and I move to a first-floor flat right next to the railway line that runs between Hampstead Heath and Gospel Oak. Standing on the balcony I watch a fox prowl the downstairs neighbour's garden in the mid-afternoon. Green ring-necked parakeets burst out of the trees overhead. Every six to eight minutes a train shoots past, shaking the bones of the building. Sometimes I feel the floorboards shudder and instinctively I hold my breath, measuring the distance between me and the doorway, thinking: is this the one we've been waiting for?

The Heath is my neat portion of wilderness; the Heath is my new home. I walk in awe under the ancient oaks. I collect red-veined leaves and tiny fallen pine cones. Wanting to be able to describe things accurately, I learn the names of trees that have featured in the pictures of stories I've read since childhood but never seen in real life. The words sound almost mythical to me now: alder, hazel, yew, ash. I look up names of birds commonly found on the Heath: siskin, coot, moorhen, redwing, mistlethrush, kestrel. They taste strange to me, like made-up words from English nursery rhymes, foreign compared to the birds I am used to: tūī, pukeko, kākā, ruru, takahē.

Po Po's name, her real name, was an English name: Mary. Did she have others? The name we called her, Po Po, is the colloquial form of wàipó, meaning *mother's mother* in Mandarin. Two characters repeated: 婆 婆. Look closer: a woman (女) and a wave (波). The three short strokes of the calligraphy brush make up a water radical, a small body of water at the edge of her, one I don't fully understand. When I write down her name I see I have drawn a woman beneath a wave, a woman in the waves.

The Pond contains layers of translucent pearls and blue-green clouds. A family of black tufted ducks floats around me as I become aware of what my body looks like: disappearing, half swallowed by the deep. There's nothing to push myself off from. I can't touch the bottom and I can't see more than a few inches under-water. I am not sure where the shape of me ends and the dark water begins. My own heart is the beating heart of the Pond. The only sure thing is my body. I hold my breath and swim out towards the place where the sun touches the surface.

The water radical 水, radical number 85 out of 214, is one of the most common in written Chinese. It forms part of thousands of characters, most of them relating to water, such as *snow, river, tears, to swim, to wash, to float, to soak.* And there are some that don't directly relate, mostly verbs: *to live, to exist, to concentrate, to mix, to strain.* Scrolling through Pleco, the free dictionary app used by Mandarin learners everywhere, I find so many water-radical words that there could be enough for an entire language of water radicals. I begin to see it. It's an inherited language, one I've carried inside me all along, one where I'm no longer perpetually caught in between. It has no distinction between past and present tense, nor between singular and plural; as a result it contains all the places I call home, as well as all my memories and all my names. I float, I strain, I swim.

Ah! to fleet /
Never fleets móre

SO MAYER

I am never more manly than when immersed in the
Kenwood Ladies' Pond.

Gerard Manley Hopkins, that is. Jesuit priest, poet
and marine insurer, Hopkins spent his schooldays at
Oakhill House, Oak Hill Way, in Oakhill Park NW3
from 1852–63, according to a black plaque erected by
the Hampstead Plaque Fund. He later taught Sunday
School ten minutes' walk away, at St John's, Hampstead
Parish Church, where he was churchwarden. Despite his
ferocious reputation – he read from the New Testament

daily at school – it's hard to imagine that Gerard (certainly as a child) never once, on a hot summer's day, took advantage of the Hampstead Heath Ponds less than half an hour's walk from his house, which had just been taken over and modernised by the New River Company, the chartered company providing drinking water for the growing villages of North London.

Like Hopkins, I went to school not far from the Heath. Our cross-country running ascended nearby Primrose Hill, another popular North London park-land, which we learned in History class had been flat land prior to being excavated as a plague pit. School swimming was indoors at the local public pool. The Ponds were for summer, for those who knew how to negotiate the Heath's unmarked paths and the Ponds' unwritten rules.

For a period in the nineties, London was divided by its telephone dialling codes. The implementation of the 07/08 prefix in 1989 may have marked the separation between the inner and outer limits of the capital but, for me, growing up on the very edge of the outer northern suburbs of the city, the Heath marked a geographical watershed: the beginning of the sanctum that was central London. Like BT's Beattie, played by Maureen Lipman in the television ads, I was a frumpy suburban Jew. Hampstead and the Heath did not mark the wild fringes – wild in both bohemian and arboreal senses – as they do for many inner-city dwellers, but instead a passport to pagan poetry and a larger secular cultural life.

Swimming in the Ponds meant, then, not swimming literally but listening; reading about the Heath. Encountering cottaging not in person, but via Armistead Maupin's *Babycakes*, the fourth of the *Tales of the City* novels, which I read wide-eyed having stolen it from WH Smiths in Paddington on a school trip to Bath, Aquae Sulis, hot spring of a Celtic water deity. And walking from Spaniard's Inn, inwards, by night thrilling to the neo-pagan rituals at the end of Marina Warner's *In a Dark Wood*. Here be myths and monsters marking my map of the Heath.

And, on my first attempt at visiting the Pond, with a cooler classmate, the summer before A levels: being greeted, while sunbathing topless, by our intimidating headmistress. Where's a plague pit to open up beneath you when you need one?

One of Hopkins' best-known poems, 'The Leaden Echo and the Golden Echo' (1882), was written to be sung by a schoolgirl choir, as part of a play the poet never finished. In it, Hopkins asks his young female singers to reflect on the brevity of earthly lives and, in particular, youth and beauty.

> Undone, done with, soon done with, and yet
>   dearly and dangerously sweet
> Of us, the wimpled-water-dimpled, not-by-
>   morning-matchèd face,
> The flower of beauty, fleece of beauty, too too
>   apt to, ah! to fleet,
> Never fleets móre, fastened with the tenderest
>   truth
> To its own best being and its loveliness of youth:
>   it is an everlastingness of, O it is an all youth!

The poem's subtitle describes it as a Maidens' Song for St Winefred's Well in Holywell, Wales. The legend of St Winifred is a cautionary tale about gender: in its bare-bones version, it tells how, in AD 660, Caradoc, the son of a local (pagan) prince, severed the head of the young Winifred after she refused to marry him, and fought off his attempt to rape her. A spring rose from the ground at the spot where her head fell, and she was later restored to life by her uncle, St Beuno. The historical Winifriede (there are over twenty variant transliterations into Latin and English of her Welsh name, Gwenffrewi) seems to have been a popular and successful noble-born abbess – 'wimpled' if not 'water-dimpled' – with a prominent scar on her neck.

Her putative refusal of Caradoc, which the historical Gwenffrewi seems to have survived, may have fused with local pre-Christian traditions about a sacred spring dedicated to a goddess like Sulis. Thus, a former female chthonic power, who perhaps granted prayers for earthly youth and beauty, gets transformed by the Church fathers into a warning against both female sexual independence and paganism. Defusing the fusion, I hear a cautionary tale about how cautionary tales get repeated in fixed patterns.

But Hopkins did not write the poem in Wales, although St Winifred's Well was then a site of pilgrimage maintained by the Jesuits. He began it in 1880, when visiting his family in London. There is – exactly – a fleeting reference to the site of his own youth and its sacred wellsprings. 'Ah! to fleet, / Never fleets móre': the repetition of 'too, too . . . to' and the sprung rhyme that lifts up the 'o' of 'móre' draws attention to the 'fleet' – or Fleet River – coursing through the poem.

Rhymed with 'sweet' it is, on the surface, a distillation of the poem's theme: mortal beauty is but an echo of the golden beauty of divinity. But the flow of 'o' drops a visual representation, not of a river (and the Fleet was, in fact, underground by the time Hopkins was walking the Heath), but of a pond; or, as on the Heath, a chain of ponds made by damming the Highgate Brook, one of the sources of the Fleet, the river that defines the North London watershed.

The ponds on the Heath were created to provide drinking water for the growing villages of Hampstead and Highgate. The iron- and mineral-rich water became known for its health-giving qualities in the late eighteenth century, turning Hampstead into a spa town; but before that, they were primarily reservoirs. The waters of the Ponds are still supposed to be maintained at drinking quality, something that any head-above-the-water swimmer in their murky, weedy green will be surprised to hear.

'Reservoir' is a sixteenth-century French word formed, unsurprisingly, from the verb 'reserver'. While we all may make (or have) reservations, the Oxford English Dictionary suggests that the initial use of the English verb 'to reserve' was ecclesiastical, meaning 'To set apart (a matter) to be dealt with by a superior authority', giving in particular a Jesuit example.

Beneath the surface of Hopkins' poem lie currents of a question, a mineral whisper that may challenge our ideas of purity: by whose authority is something sacred? How does a cautionary tale persist, or myth grow up? What lies in reserve in the waters in which we regard ourselves? And have we forgotten that water is sacred in itself, and kept sacred by our regard for it, a regard arising from our molecular need for hydration?

As Kuntala Lahiri-Dutt writes in her book *Fluid Bonds: Views on Gender and Water*:

> The purificatory power of water, to wash away all pollution, all sin, all physical filth, is an essential feature in the religious symbolism in societies. This quality does not arise because of its intrinsic purity but because it absorbs pollution and carries it away.

Just as St Winifred's Well, which is mentioned in the chivalric Middle English poem *Sir Gawain and the Green Knight*, can then be thought of as the wellspring of a certain line of British mystic landscape poetry, so the Heath, as North London's watershed, seems to have drawn visionary poets. According to Tom Bolton in *London's Lost Rivers*:

> This path [Millfield Lane, which runs alongside the Ladies' Pond] was a regular and favourite walk of Samuel Taylor Coleridge, who lived in Highgate. He once met John Keats here by chance, and shook his hand, accurately commenting to his companion, 'There is death in that hand.'

According to the second volume of Richard Holmes' biography of Coleridge, *Darker Reflections*, Keats remembered a longer conversation *in situ* with Coleridge that day in 1819, which included a discussion of the poet Robert Southey's belief in 'mermaids', those sirens of eternal feminine youth and undying loveliness who could be seen as a green-gold echo of the fleeting beauties and their soul-damning seductions which Hopkins set swimming in the watery reflections of his poem.

In 'The Leaden Echo and the Golden Echo' it is not the poet himself who looks into the still waters of St Winifred's Well, but a young woman. In doing this, Hopkins fuses the figure of Echo – 'the girl with no door on her mouth,' as Anne Carson calls her in her essay 'The Gender of Sound' – with her beloved Narcissus, the beautiful son of a nymph who, in the same story, falls silent and dies contemplating his own beauty in the surface of a pool. The Greek myth is, among other things, a cautionary tale about gender: Echo's persuasive speech is a conventionally masculine quality, while Narcissus' obsession with his beauty is conventionally feminine.

Narcissus is punished by dying, but the punishment is mediated both by the fact that he dies young and leaves a good-looking corpse, and that he rises up as the narcissus, whereas Echo is punished for both her desire and her speech, by losing her voice and fading into nothing at all but the word for being secondary. Fusing them, Hopkins creates – imagines – a silent, rapt Echo regarding herself; she is a hybrid, like a mermaid, half Echo and half Narcissus; half Gerard Manley Hopkins, and half the schoolgirls that he imagined singing the poem.

Just before the legion of cis male Romantic poets walked the Heath (although of course Keats was sometimes accompanied by milliner and textile artist Fanny Brawne), a defining presence walked there. Although she would have been unlikely to swim in any of the ponds, she could be seen as a mermaid, as she was regarded by her society as a hybrid: Dido Elizabeth Belle (Lindsay), who lived at Kenwood House from 1765–95, was the daughter of Maria Belle, an enslaved African woman in the British West Indies, and British naval officer Sir John Lindsay. Lindsay's uncle, the first Earl of Mansfield and owner of Kenwood House, raised her as a freedwoman, a member of an aristocratic family and as companion to their other great-niece, Lady Elizabeth Murray. As teenagers, Belle and Elizabeth were painted together by Scottish artist David Martin, in the first European painting to depict a black subject on an equal eye-line with a white subject – although until the 1990s the painting (attributed to Johann Zoffany) was known as 'The Lady Elizabeth Murray', and the other figure in the painting was described as 'a servant'. The painting, which now hangs at the Earl of Mansfield's ancestral home of Scone Castle, used to hang in Kenwood.

Amma Asante's biopic *Belle* (2013) contains a wordless scene that shows Belle struggling to find her reflection in a society that rendered her invisible and wanted only to erase her, an erasure that continued almost to the present day. In the scene, Belle looks at herself in the mirror after a bruising confrontation in the household, and pulls at her skin. It is a rare private moment in a film that plays out in the public spheres of both the drawing rooms of Jane Austen's marriage plots, and the stately and bloodless spaces of the law courts, whose law lords have the blood of millions of enslaved and murdered Africans on their hands. Belle does not have the privilege of Hopkins' imagined Victorian schoolgirls, most likely white and middle-class, to imagine herself as a universal image of beauty and youth, although – as Martin's painting shows clearly – she was a woman of great beauty, poise, mischief, determination and intelligence, all captured by Gugu Mbatha-Raw's award-winning on-screen performance.

A decade after Dido Elizabeth Belle arrived at Kenwood House, in 1777, the Hampstead Water

Company drained a malarial marsh on the Heath to add to the drinking water reservoirs. Fifteen years later, just before Belle left the house to marry abolitionist John Davinier, the picturesque Thousand Pound Pond (also known as the Concert Pond, but initially named for its huge expense) was dug. In between, her great-uncle famously ruled on the Zong case, determining that slavery had never been legal in English common law and that there would be no insurance payout to the slavers who had murdered enslaved people on board the British ship *Zong*. At the same time as she worked to enact vast social and political change, Belle would have been witness to change on a far smaller scale in front of her house. I wonder if she might have seen a reflection of herself, finally, within her society, and within the waters of the newly created Concert Pond.

When we think about reflections and mirrors, we think about Narcissus, about beauty and perfection – and perhaps about the cautionary tale of their siren seductions. But Belle's gaze into the Concert Pond gives us another possibility. Just as there is a 'leaden Echo and a golden Echo' in Hopkins' poem, could there also be a 'leaden Narcissus'? Golden Narcissus, the privileged son of a goddess who has nothing to do but contemplate his own perfection, nothing to attach himself to the world, has another side; and this underside might be like the philosophical weight that Hopkins finds in his echo. Instead of a fleeting narcissism: everything that we as historical bodies swim in. Everything we press down on or bear up on – our gravity and the heavy feelings that buoy us into a false fantasy of floating, lightness.

Sinking into ourselves, like a leaden Narcissus, might sound painful – and lead is, of course, a poison, especially when dissolved in water. Lead concentrate levels in London drinking water are now negligible, but only after twenty years of concerted campaigning by the British Medical Association to bring the UK government's 'action' level down. The lead pipes that brought water from the Heath reservoirs, part of huge Victorian civic infrastructure projects, have slowly been replaced.

Minerals are often a body of water's memory of the rocks it courses through; they are a *pharmakon*, a cure or a poison, because they linger in living bodies, too. The leaden Narcissus, then, is the full and complicated weight of our history, a reflection that sinks below the surface, taking on – and in – all that water. When we look, or leap, into the frondy gymslip-green cold-as-is-good-for-you water of the Ladies' Pond, we move through the tangles of history, the taste of molecular memory. We gulp down Hopkins' spit and sweat and piss, and we step out of the water shedding Dido Belle's skin cells, torn in her attempt to conform to her society's narrow expectations.

This essay's diversions into history, into poetry, are not waterborne contemplations. I don't swim at the Ladies' Pond any more because it is too painful to do so. It's not just the memory of being caught sunbathing topless there by my headmistress (she was unfazed, I was drowning in shame), it's that my body wasn't comfortable with being assigned female then, and it isn't now.

So, some of that lead is my own poison: the full and complicated weight of my flesh, in all its shames and awkwardness, its hairiness and bulges, its exposures and limitations, its breathlessness and chronic pain, its discomfort in the deeply impractical, un-body-shaped stuff that passes for swimwear, and with negotiating binary gender and gender essentialism.

It feels, these days, that even the mallards and moorhens seem to police gender with the beady gaze of their Jesuitical authority. External protestors disrupting a recent Kenwood Ladies' Pond Association meeting about allowing transwomen swimmers to continue using the Ladies' Pond (as they long have) wore the WOMEN ONLY sign from the Pond gate around their necks, a grotesque invocation of slave auctions only feet from where Belle and the Earl of Mansfield fought for emancipation. It gives me reservations about the Pond as a community; gives me literally, a sinking feeling; heavy as lead.

Hopkins, rooting himself however unconsciously in his childhood, reminds us that however much we consider our (shameful, exclusionary) pasts, both personal and political, 'Undone, done with, soon done with', they remain. What seems 'to fleet' is actually what stays: the river is still, just, visible at points on the Heath as it is not anywhere else in London. In Hopkins' Jesuit theology, it is earthly life that fleets while divinity remains; but in the poem it is his – and our – thought and language that is fleet. It is swift, but its swiftness, thought compressed by the urgency of time, is its staying power.

Swimming is a dip into ritual time, the time of repetition, of the elemental; but also a reminder of historical time: its continuities, and how its cautionary tales continue to make us cautious; of being different; of being hybrid; of not conforming. We keep ourselves in reserve, as I have been doing from the Pond. But I know I am not alone: there are many trans and non-binary people who swim, and have swum, in the Ladies' Pond. Their molecules and their courage are already coursing through the water like minerals, feeding the daffodils – those golden narcissi – that grow in such abundance around Kenwood House in spring, hidden springs surfacing.

Summer

Out of Time

MARGARET DRABBLE

I lived in Hampstead, just off South End Green, from 1968 to the mid-1990s, and these were the happiest years of my life. It was a good time to be there, and we were lucky to be so near to the Heath and the Pond. I've always loved to swim, ever since my father patiently taught me in the cold salt waves of the North Sea off the Yorkshire coast. I even enjoyed visits to the echoing and heavily chlorinated Glossop Road public baths in Sheffield, now the site of a Wetherspoons. So when we moved to Hampstead, I was delighted to find myself within walking distance of the Kenwood Ladies' Bathing Pond. It was a lovely walk, past the lower Mixed Pond (where we once secretly released from its plastic bag an unhappy goldfish which we had won at

the fair) and up over the brow of the Heath towards
Kenwood. I used to walk regularly to Kenwood, to
look at the house and the paintings and the Henry
Moore statue and Samuel Johnson's summer house,
but I was a fair-weather swimmer, and went to the
Pond only on good days in the summer. I heard tales of
the legendary characters who swam all the year round,
well into their eighties, but I never aspired to be one
of them. Summer was my time.

I used to know the Heath so well, but on my last
visit to find the Pond I managed to get myself thor-
oughly lost. There was a joy in this as well as a sadness.
All walks on the Heath are beautiful, and in the
resplendent summer of 2018 they were more beautiful
than ever, and there was no danger of losing oneself
for long. I wandered along paths and avenues and past
many a vast and fallen oak lying hugely on its side.
The trees of the Heath always make me think of John
Keats, who lived so near, and who must have known
them well. ('Those green-robed senators of mighty
woods', I often mutter to myself in woodland, in
homage to Keats.) And there, eventually, I came upon
the tree-encircled pool, which manages to stay secret
and concealed although it is so well attended. Many
memories came back to me as I wondered whether to
perch on the ladder and dip a toe into the soft clear
brown water. As it happened, I didn't dare. There were

too many people queuing up to take the plunge and I didn't want to get in their way. I felt old and nervous. It wasn't like that in the old days.

I'm not sure if I ever went with my daughter, as small children weren't allowed into the enclosure and it was good to be in a child-free zone for a while. In her teens my daughter became a much stronger swimmer than I ever was, and she often went to the Pond with her friends, but I usually went alone, with a book and sometimes a sandwich. In the seventies, some of us sunbathed topless, which was officially frowned upon, though the lifeguards usually turned a blind eye. I went once or twice with an older lesbian friend who had once been a Cistercian nun, and, briefly, a nudist: I don't think she liked swimming but she liked the ambience, with its strange mixture of permissiveness and purity. But I loved to lower myself down the rungs of the ladder and launch myself into the silky waters of the Pond. There was something magical about the unplumbed depths, the moorhens, the dragonflies, the waterlilies, the willows, the floating rings and rafts. It was timeless, though perhaps the period it most evoked (despite the bikinis and the hippy beads) was Edwardian: it was the female equivalent of that fine bathing party scene in E. M. Forster's *A Room with a View*, where the Reverend Mr Beebe and George Emerson and young Freddy cast off their clothes and

disport themselves in a village pool in the mild landscape of Surrey.

In my novel, *The Pure Gold Baby*, I set a scene of
perfect happiness at the Ladies' Pond. Anna, the protag-
onist's daughter, now a young woman, is an eager
swimmer, and Jessica, reading Proust, keeps half an eye
on her as she lies on the grassy bank. 'She sees the
fringe of sallows and elders, she hears the slow strokes
of an elderly stout swimmer, the ripple of water, the
faint hum of hoverflies, the murmurs of conversation.
The pond and the little lake stretch timelessly towards
infinity. Out of time, all is well for the ageing mother
and the ageless daughter.'

This is a fictitious memory, but it stands in for many
good and peaceful hours. But I also recall a dramatic
and frightening visit to the Pond. I must, unusually,
have driven over, I can't think why. I wouldn't know
how to do that now, and would have no idea where to
park. I think I must have parked on leafy Millfield Lane,
and it must have been summer. I remember walking
towards the Pond with my bathing things, and realising
that a sudden storm was brewing. Why hadn't I noticed
it before? There were flashes of lightning, tremendous
claps of thunder, and then, without much warning,
torrential rain began to fall. I knew that swimming in
stormy weather was dangerous and so decided to turn
back towards my car. By this time the rain was pouring

down in a deluge and forked lightning continued to streak the sky. When I got back to the car, soaked through, I didn't know whether it would be safe to get into it or not. Was I safer standing out in the open? Should I even touch the car? If I got into it, would the rubber tyres earth the car and protect me? (They wouldn't – that's a myth.) I can't remember what I did but I remember standing there thinking I was a bloody fool to be there in the first place. It was an apocalyptic moment. I know now that getting into the water would have been a very dangerous and stupid thing to do though I am sure the ever-watchful lifeguards would have whistled everybody out in no time.

I enjoy storms, on the whole, and am not predisposed to fear them. This one was unforgettable and unnerving, but it wasn't as extreme as the Hampstead storm of 1975, which I missed as I was away on holiday. On 14 August, so much rain fell on the Heath in three hours that the downpour has been classified as a once-in-every-20,000-years event. I was sorry to have missed the drama, and heard much about it from friends and neighbours when I got home. Urban legend had it that so much water flowed down the steps into the underground public toilets at South End Green that somebody was drowned down there, but that's certainly not true. There seems to have been only one death indirectly linked with the flood. But that didn't prevent a much-contested and successfully resisted move to re-landscape the ponds to prevent future 'dam collapse' and 'life loss'. Opponents of the threatened City of London scheme acknowledged that as the ponds were artificially created, they needed to be artificially maintained, but they also pointed out that human history on the Heath hadn't existed for more than 20,000 years, so a similarly devastating flood wasn't likely to happen again very soon.

In those Hampstead days of my youth I hadn't realised that the ponds, although they look so natural, were created centuries ago (possibly as early as 1692) by the damming of two streams that arose in the Heath. The streams, according to *Taking the Waters: A Swim Around Hampstead Heath* (2012) by Caitlin Davies, 'then join in Camden Town to form the River Fleet, which in turn flows through London and joins the Thames'. The Fleet is one of those great London rivers that has been almost wholly buried below ground in sewer systems, and I've never been quite sure of its original course: it seemed in wet weather to flow through our cellar on its way to join what I guess must have been its main current beneath Fleet Road, before it went on its way through Camden and Kentish Town to the grander regions of Fleet Street. There is something enthralling about underground rivers, even when they have been tamed and flow through manmade pipes.

We like to think of the watery world hidden beneath us. One of U.A. Fanthorpe's best known poems, 'Rising Damp', celebrates these rivers and acknowledges their unruly power.

> At our feet they lie low
> The little fervent underground
> Rivers of London
>
> *Effra, Graveney, Falcon, Quaggy*
> *Wandle, Walbrook, Tyburn, Fleet*

They are boxed in and have gone under, she writes, but they 'return spectrally after heavy rain' to confound suburban gardens, deluge cellars, and detonate manholes. The landscape is alive, and the rivers at times resurgent.

It makes me happy to remember that I once used to swim in the source of a great and historic river. It gives me a sense of retrospective empowerment, as though I had been in touch with the pagan gods of streams and brooks and fountains. I still know people who swim there, every week, all the year round. The lifeguards tell me that the ponds are more valued now than ever, as London entertainments grow ever more expensive, and our need for some contact with the natural world more imperative. They are well protected by those who love them. It is a small miracle that they have survived so well for so long.

The Lifeguard's Perspective

NELL FRIZZELL

Sitting on my wildly yellow canoe, six months pregnant, my son kicking a tango against my ribs, I look down at the shallow waters and see a shoal of roach flit past; their red fins and tail frills a thrill against the silt pond floor. All around me, women bob and splash – decapitated heads in a mud-coloured wash – with absolutely no idea of the throng flitting beneath their bellies. They can't see the fish, the reeds, the swan mussels. That is the lifeguard's perspective alone. It is the lifeguards, the faintly ridiculous figures in sun-lolly outfits of red shorts and yellow vests, who get to look down into the pond from above; a slanted look into the depths. It is the lifeguards who stand for ten hours at a time, in a heatwave, in rain, over ice, and observe the wildlife, the mischief and human drama that unfolds across this tiny and yet enormous pond.

From the lifeguard's perspective you see everything: on the banks, in the water, in the trees and across the surrounding meadows. You see the crayfish, moor chicks, abandoned bras, the half-eaten Waitrose picnics splayed across the ground like victims of a disembowelling, the dropped credit cards, the smears and coke cans it is our responsibility to clean up, the hawks bathing in the shallows, the owls hooting before the sun rises, the mist, the ice, the floating plasters and gold rings.

I am a poacher-turned-gamekeeper; a swimmer-turned-lifeguard. Two years ago I got a tap on the shoulder from one of my great and enduring heroes: a lifeguard, bodger, artist and inspiration called Jane Smith who has been working at the Pond for over seven years. It was a thick winter day, grey and silent, and I had just swum a lap wondering, as I so often wonder, why I do this. 'Would you be interested in being a lifeguard?' she asked. This is how, at eight weeks pregnant, I found myself in a training pool in central London, awash with morning sickness, learning how to tow, lift, administer first aid and otherwise rescue those in need. Before telling my own mother I was pregnant I'd confessed it to a room full of Lycra-clad strangers. They let me off some of the heavier lifting. I tried not to throw up when they ate tuna for lunch.

As a lifeguard, I have been educated in a side of the Pond that, as a swimmer, I had never known. The wildlife, the women and the wild night-time goings on. One morning I paddled out to see an enormous, elliptical shell nestled on the shallow pond floor. This, Jane informed me, was a swan mussel: a fresh water mussel that cleans, every day, hundreds of litres of water. She calls them jewels; their iridescent interiors the stuff of Pacific island dreams. There are the crayfish – not native but like tiny lobsters – the dragonflies, the bream, the kingfisher and the enormous, near-spherical carp. Towards the end of that pregnant summer one of the carp, an older lady we christened Carole, came up to the surface. She was probably ill, moving towards the end of her life with a flash of fame; literally a moment in the sun. Swimmers were terrified. There were screams, yelps, cries for help. People confused Carole with a snake, a shark, an old car tyre, an abandoned motorbike – even a dead body. Looking at her bloated, ungainly progress across the Pond, and feeling my own girth spread ever thicker, I felt a certain sympathy. Until Carole came along, I'd got away with telling children that there were no fish in the Pond. Now I was forced to admit that, yes, three metres down, in the silty, smelly depths there are carp without number, some rather large indeed, swimming about like they own the place.

'Are there pike in here?' I would be asked, several times a shift, as I floated in the lily pads, watching the water, occasionally shouting at some swimmer that lying on a life ring may well cost an asthmatic her life. I would usually lie and say definitely not. The truth, as Jane once let slip after a particularly long, gruelling shift, is that there's everything you can imagine in the Pond. There are water snakes, some of them three feet long. There are slow worms, tiny copper-bellied fellows that bury their bodies in the damp corners and the drains. When I asked Jane about the strangest thing she'd ever found at the Pond, the answer shocked even me: a seven-foot reticulated python about three feet from the upper meadow. 'It would have been dumped, I suppose, by someone who realised that a seven-foot reticulated python could actually eat you,' she laughs. 'It was just metres from where people sunbathe on the meadow. It had been living there; it had made a nest. But the cold must have got it, in the end.'

It was standing on the unyielding concrete of the deck, for hours at a time, that Jane taught me how to read the weather. There are often two layers of cloud above the Heath, she explained; a higher and lower. If they're both going in the same direction then the weather will stay the same. If they're moving in different directions then the weather will change. This is how, on a bright, sunny day, I would know that it was going to rain later. I learned about the structure of the Pond; about the deep, S-shaped stream that runs through its centre, sometimes five feet below the surface; about the chain of ponds that flow down from the spring by Kenwood – women, boating, men, dogs, in that order; about the River Fleet that supposedly runs under but probably leaks into our pond; about the need to clean the thick, glossy, putrid-smelling sludge of leaves, mud, bird shit and hair that gathers at the shallow outflow; of the currents that run beneath the swimmers' feet; of the need to maintain the proper ratio of lifeguards on duty to swimmers in the water, no matter how furious those waiting may become.

I also learned, as I grew a little life inside me, about human nature. I saw women stripped bare by the cold and the wet. I became able to spot the grief-stricken, the ill, the heartbroken. I would see them transformed, sometimes. I saw the pure, buoyant joy of a physically disabled woman who swam the entire length of the Pond without anyone noticing. I watched people arrive on mobility scooters, with sticks, on crutches, with prosthetic limbs or pacemakers and swim without the tiniest need of my assistance. I watched healthy, young, fit women turned rigid by the water, with terror at there being no bottom, by their own undisclosed inability to swim, and felt my heart leap into my mouth as I ran to save them. As I scrubbed piss off the floor or shit off the toilets, I learned that women can be disgusting. As I was given advice on everything from how to move a breech baby to what it's like to hit The Barry Manipause, I learned that women can be wonderful. As I walked down the rust-coloured path each morning, the bushes and fences festooned with lacy knickers, hot pink bras, greying shorts and sensible white briefs, I learned that midnight passion can break in many forms.

As a lifeguard, I learned that home is no one place and that nostalgia can bloom like chlorophyll. 'I almost cried when I was taught how to make the straw sausages,' explains Jane, describing the little hay-like floats that are strung along behind the boundary ropes. 'You see, I realised that we were using barley straw and my grandad grew barley. Not many people do. Here I was, working in north London with bales of straw, just as I had as a child on the farm.' As it decomposes, barley straw releases a substance that changes the acidity in the Pond, which means that toxic blue-green algaes cannot bloom. They're brilliant, but for one particular lifeguard, those funny straw sausages strung across the end rope, buoyed up with empty plastic bottles, can also be a time machine. For me, the bob and sway of the rowing boat in the corner of the Pond, its oars requisitioned into a

nest for the moorhen and her chicks, its bow occasionally tapping against the fence, its stern against the hoist,
acted as a time machine to my riverside childhood in
Oxford. It reminded me of a rat, not one that eats goose
eggs and scavenges in bins beside abandoned towels,
but of the *Wind in the Willows* hero that can think of
nothing – absolutely nothing – half so much worth
doing as simply messing about in boats.

I saw women slip off their bikinis in the middle
of the Pond when they thought nobody was looking;
I saw women swim down as far as their lungs would
allow, darkening and disappearing in the brown silty
water; I watched tufted ducks dive with feathers full of
air bubbles; I watched couples hang off the boundary
ropes and kiss lazily, for hours, unaware or unconcerned
about the hundreds of hot, fractious women queuing
in the afternoon sun, waiting for them to get out so
there was room for others to get in; I saw unwary
tourists stand at the fence and admire the scene, only
to get screamed at by swimmers protective of their
privacy; I witnessed women sulk like toddlers when
told they could not swim naked.

On that steaming solstice afternoon, as I lolled in the
water on my gaudy yellow board, I remembered my
first trimester as a lifeguard, when I would have to run,

hand clasped over my mouth, to the bin I dragged to the entrance of our office each day. I would hunch over, my eyes still on the water, and throw up as quietly as possible. To this day I still wonder if a single swimmer ever noticed. Somehow, as a lifeguard, you are cartoonishly visible – with your yellow jumper, your red whistle and your big white chair – and simultaneously invisible; just another piece of equipment like the life rings, the ladder or the hoist. A swimmer's focus will always be, should always be, on the Pond; that strange surface dance between the submerged and the open air world.

But after dark, as the thousands of women that have passed through the gate finally make their way home, as the pink sky turns to inky grey, as the surface of the Pond falls still and silent; that is when we take back our pond. As night falls, we slip into the water and swim out across the mirror. As the water turns black in the dimming light, we open our eyes beneath the surface and suddenly we're not swimmers anymore, but astronauts; star sailors. We are floating through a silky, thick black, as bottomless as the night sky.

Echolocation

SHARLENE TEO

It's late morning in the middle of August; big sun a bully at the height of its power. 'You think of your toe only when you stub it,' goes one of my favourite quotes from Akhil Sharma. I like what it suggests about different parts of the body being individuated by pain or shock. Right now I am fully focused on the vulnerability of my toes in the freezing green water of the Kenwood Ladies' Pond. With the anxious hyper-awareness of a first-timer I think about snagging the sole of my foot on a shard of glass or kicking a fish in the face. Even on a hot day the water is so cold that it shucks me out of my skin. I feel boneless, just a mass of nerves and gooseflesh girded in someone's skeleton.

Keep moving to stay warm. This directive sounds like life advice. After a while I start to drift in the appeal of it. Lately, I keep coming across essays about the proven mental and physical benefits of wild swimming. It seems both timeless and like the in-thing. Even though no one's watching I feel self-conscious and out of place. I always tell people I'm a city mouse. That is my euphemism for a lack of wildness, a constant pawing for Wi-Fi and fizzy water. I have never had to struggle to survive. I know I wouldn't last long in the truest outdoors. I'd probably die of exposure and get eaten by animals.

To my left are two women in their mid-fifties wearing swimming caps. They remind me collectively of Esther, a German dramaturge I met in 2017, a powerful lady who dives in the same Berlin lake every morning at the whip-crack of dawn. The scene is chicly bucolic, both Instagrammable and matter-of-fact, unshowy. The mostly white women sunning themselves on the banks and in the water take up as much space as they want to, no more, no less. The atmosphere is one of tranquil matrilineal kinship; there's no frisson of casually charged watchfulness or the sexually competitive energy that you'd get in a mixed environment, say, in a packed beach or festival lake. There's none of the blokey showmanship (bro-manship?) and pectoral posturing you get from some men in other parts of the Heath. I understand now why there's a cult of sisterhood around the Pond. I wish I could claim I frequented it before it became fashionable, but it is the recently ubiquitous recommendations of acquaintances and a glowing *Vice* article that have finally led me here.

Now that I've acclimatised I move forward with greater ease. If I close my eyes my proximity to London becomes a matter of guesswork and echolocation. Bats use echolocation to find their way around and hunt in the dark. They create ultrasonic sound waves and the returning echoes enable them to detect obstacles or prey. It is a common misconception that bats are blind, but I like the poetic conceit of echolocation. Of not being able to see what's ahead, but nonetheless constantly moving; both vulnerable and on high alert, sending out signals and listening out for echoes that situate where you are and how to keep on going.

Drifting forward I can hear crickets, ducks, water, female voices low and indistinct, and something buzzing overhead. Behind my eyelids summertime unspools into its various sticky components. The news cycle is a hell fire and like most people I can't stop worrying about the future. I want to write fiction forever, but this seems unsustainable on a practical, financial level. The more seriously I take it the less competent I feel. Everything is a wobble. Pressingly and depressingly, I am not quite in love but not quite out of love with a not quite partner who convolutes more than vivifies my life. Howdy, partner. I think of two gunmen facing off, arms akimbo, fists clenched over holsters. If I somehow settled those quiet fights and cagey feelings – if I cleared out the armoury of a relationship, a career – what am I left with?

Having no idea, I busy my body with what's physical. I stick to breaststroke. Front crawl I'll leave to the chlorinated clarity of a public pool, in which line floats encourage a performative discipline, alternating styles with each length, rhythmic patternation. Isn't it nicer to lead with parting palms than loping forward, catching a breath near your armpit? A pond or lake is an environment more conducive to floating or dawdling, to taking it as easy as you like. Without the pressure of a lane mate, it feels so much more convivial yet comfortably solitary in here.

'London has a particular way of making you feel like a failure,' a close friend recently said. She moved to Berlin three years ago. Even though she had, for all intents and purposes, a successful London life, the perimeters of what this city stood for had started to bore and disillusion her. London makes and unmakes trends and expectations through its ever-evolving cosmopolitan mythos, the pomp and pressure of a cultural capital. Visiting the Pond is a validating experience that resides both within and without this mythology. There's a wholesomely escapist quality to being at the Pond, somewhere between a good yoga class and being caught up in the sweeping romanticism of a Merchant Ivory film. It reminds me, the foreign first-timer, of a kind of rosy-cheeked, robust bohemian Englishness. Throughout my Singaporean adolescence, impressions of this Englishness seeped into my post-colonial imagination through classic novels and sumptuous period dramas, powerful cultural transmissions which seemed representative of a whole, both distinctive and distancing. Blissfully nostalgic, this Englishness centred upon the charmingly tumultuous lives of the white upper and middle classes, where passion was conveyed in clipped accents and even dishevelment was tasteful, just a transient mode and not a given. A character like the nobly beautiful, barefooted Topaz from Dodie Smith's *I Capture the Castle* would fit right in here, I think. I feel very foreign in how much I overthink simply occupying such a friendly, liberal space. Maybe it's symptomatic of anhedonia or my overall anxious condition.

On one hand the Pond signifies a return to offline pleasure, the humbly gorgeous ways in which nature can comfort, console or entertain. On the other hand, being here feels like checking an item off on a bucket list of verified belonging, one step closer to integrating into this vaunted capital that I've felt contentedly isolated in for nine years. You know you're a city person when you make a big deal out of a pocket of nature. The Pond is a transporting haven away from the crush of actual transportation, from pushy men and push notifications, from smog and trash and blister-giving shoes.

For most of the past decade I was preoccupied to the point of anguish with trying to stay in England. Getting my visa and work situation organised was not just a practical pursuit but also an existential one. What does the right to remain signify but the desire to keep being the person you are still in the process of becoming, in the conditions you find most conducive to your development? If I paid my taxes and made an honest living, what else did I have to justify? Yet things are never as simple as that, and they keep getting more complicated. Both politically, in terms of a tense national climate and tightening immigration legislation, as well as in the individual context of how, for some, ageing involves the accrual of a more bruised and complex conscience; one littered with a litany of regrets, what-ifs and second-guesses.

Back in those grey-area years I often felt like a straggler, a privileged cockroach clinging on for dear, parasitic life. I found serious dating difficult, loaded as it was with the threat and impetus of time-sensitive

marriage. Hovering over the vagaries of a relationship: the finitude of a visa expiry date. The intricate
impersonality of immigration paperwork, designed to
daunt, with its painfully personal implications. I was
constantly in the process of proving the legality of my
existence. Not knowing how long you'll get to stay
in the city you want to live in feels like travelling half
blind, like sending a sound wave across a canyon.

If Singapore, the country I come from, is a perfectly
nice place, why did I want, so adamantly, to stay in
London? At the time, my answer was obvious. London
was the city where I gained what Gustave Flaubert
termed my sentimental education – those wobbling
steps taken in the early twenties toward empathy and
something approaching wisdom, or at least the softly
cynical benefit of hindsight. If I went back to Singapore
I was worried I'd regress into the more babyish person
I'd worked hard to outgrow.

When I moved to London in 2009 I still printed out
Google maps to get around. I lived between Stockwell
and Clapham North in a filthy flat full of mould and
mice. Almost everyone I know from out of London has
a similarly squalid origin story, some nightmare flat-
mates or disgusting conditions that furnish a narrative
of habituating to the city. After a shaky beginning, you
settle into one corner of a borough and come to know
it well, experiencing a kind of hard-won, grumpy

tenderness toward a certain corner shop or small cafe. You brandish location-centric in-jokes with pride and scoff at dawdling tourists. It's hard to familiarise yourself with a different neighbourhood to the same degree of thoroughness and intimacy unless multiple loved ones reside there. I have never lived in convenient proximity to Hampstead Heath. That's my excuse for why I can count the number of occasions I've been to it on both hands. Each time, I skirted the periphery of the Pond, aware of its feted, beatific existence but constantly putting off a swim myself. The top of Parliament Hill issued a clarion call to someone's birthday or leaving do, some difficult or serious conversation to be had, cheap wine and sweating snacks to be consumed on pilling blankets. There was always somewhere else to be and someone more certain to become. I told myself that one day when I comfortably belonged and didn't have to worry about the right to remain, I could take the time to discover every unfamiliar part of London with a leisurely complacency.

It's been almost two years since my visa issues were finally settled and the binder containing every payslip, bank statement and qualification I ever earned gathers dust somewhere in the flat that I can now live in with relative certainty. The big worry that dogged most of my twenties no longer undercuts everything, yet it is replaced by another kind of question – now that

I have gotten to stay, why can't I reside happily in a happy ending? A woman swimming past gives me a smile. The atmosphere is so peaceful and lovely but I'm getting fidgety. I have that dark dawning feeling in the back of my head: the memory of some indistinct task I haven't completed, someone I've crossed, something urgent to do. With no clock to hand I have no idea how long I have spent in the water. I clamber out ungracefully and towel off, in a hurry, already, to find my way home.

Landmarks

AMY KEY

Take care whom you mix with in life,
  irresponsible one,
For if you mix with the wrong people
– And you yourself may be one of the
  wrong people –
If you make love to the wrong person,
              [. . .]
They will do you ferocious, indelible harm!
              —Rosemary Tonks, 'Done for!'

At some point in my late thirties it struck me that
perhaps I was 'one of the wrong people'. My personal
wrongness: a kind of self-sabotage that had let 'the
wrong people' in and was compounded by my own,

innate wrongness. My mission became *find a way to protect your self, from your self.* My hunch was this could be achieved through a kind of unimpeachable stability in my life. Stability in this sense was chiefly about control: eight hours' sleep each night, no disordering crushes (no letting in the 'wrong people'), avoidance of breaking news, a kind of magical delusion regarding difficult relationships in my life, eating all the fresh food in the fridge,* stockpiling the emblems of self-care and responsible household management (Waitrose Essentials Pink Grapefruit Bath Foam, bin liners, salted butter, toilet roll). If I maintained a state of vigilance, nothing could shake me. If I let one of those things slip, then everything else might follow. Like when a person coughs during a performance, and all the other coughs, contained until that moment, escape and expose their owner.

I was about to turn forty. My friends told me that their own run-ups to this milestone felt terrible. A kind of inner weather that didn't let your leaves settle. Afterwards, they said, they felt OK. This is what kept

---

*Yesterday I took a cucumber from the salad tray of the fridge and as I tightened my grip on it, its insides gave way; became a dank mush inside the shrink-wrapped plastic. I gagged as I tried to ease it out into the compost bin, eventually taking a pair of scissors and cutting into the wrapper, like an A&E doctor cutting through clothing to treat a patient. At what point had the cucumber lost itself, and why did I not get to it sooner?

me going from the moment I turned thirty-nine and trudged towards the finish line.

I'd sold some poems to the American magazine *Poetry*. I decided I would use the money to buy myself a ring. I commissioned a huge faceted opal held in gold pigeon claws. A forty-year old woman in control of her life would buy herself a ring, I thought. Opals are fragile and if faceted, they are more so. 'What happens if it breaks?' I asked the jeweller. 'We'll deal with that if and when it happens,' she said – 'you just have to love it and wear it.' Fear for the future of the opal on my finger nibbled away at my pleasure – perhaps it was an act of self-sabotage to incorporate such fragility into my daily routine; after all, wasn't I a calamity, a person forever bruised and scratched by their own careless-ness? I loved the opal, its galactic flashes of colour, but could I handle the precarity I'd chosen?

I also promised myself that I would swim in every body of water I encountered during that year. In water I felt more expert in my body – could achieve a flexibility of thought that grew towards compassion. Directing my compassion inwards created a little air pocket of optimism, a kind of buffer zone of comfort; this was what water gave me. Mostly I kept to my promise – swimming in tiny hotel pools, lakes, rocky rivers, Mediterranean beaches, lidos, the brisk sea at Ramsgate on the last day of my thirties – except when in South Shields at Christmas, where I stood alone on the shore, my hood pulled up, having left my family to squabble indoors.

In my early twenties I lived in a mansion block overlooking Parliament Hill Lido. I never swam there. I walked on the Heath most weekends, the hem of my jeans soaking up mud and rain. I never swam in the ponds. Of all the missed opportunities in my life this one still scratches at me. I was afraid of the cold, of my body being seen. And at that time I did not know how to float.*

---

* I learned to float aged twenty-six when I went to stay with some friends in France at the invitation of an old friend of mine, Adam. Adam's mum and her partner owned a tall terraced house in a very small village that is arranged alongside a river that has deep, cascading pools at the foot of huge, forested hills. We would walk up the river to a spot that had large flat stones we could lie down on to sunbathe, before jumping into the incredibly cold, still water of the plunge pool. I'd rarely been abroad and this was a transformative holiday for me. The plunge pool was too small for real swimming so to comfortably stay in the water, and feel as though the courage it had taken to jump in had paid off, I had to float. At first, I used a pool noodle to support my body in the water. I was unreasonably aggrieved by the aesthetic of that so when a friend got into the pool too, I eased it from under my body, offering it to them instead. I lay on my back and closed my eyes, with my arms outstretched, hands raking through the water as though it was something supple. As soon as I realised I was keeping afloat with little effort I panicked and reached for the edge of the pool. By the end of that day I'd mastered floating, the sun had burned only the upside of my body. This was the

A few months before my birthday I booked a flight to Phú Quốc, an island off the coast of Vietnam. I told myself this was my reward for staying the course. All those bodies of water, all those ways of being held (sometimes I imagine the water as a kind of memory foam mattress that yields to hold my body, to support me) would now be made available to me. I'd decided the sea was the medium by which I could arrive at an integrated, unalterable self. Water has this way of reinforcing the resilience and determination of the body – the body's objective is to keep you breathing. Water has a way of disembodying too – once in the water, your body hardly matters – you're all consciousness.

I arrived in Phú Quốc exhausted; a cold was coming on. I didn't feel excitement on the flight, I felt I was enduring, as though I'd badly planned my week and left no time for rest. I'd bagged a whole row of seats to myself, but even so, I didn't sleep except in mean little gasps.

I stayed at a small beach resort on the north of the island. When I arrived I was given a freshly squeezed passion fruit juice, I drank it like a cure. I spent the first

---

year I started to write poetry. I returned home with an ecstatic image of jumping into the pool and the surface cracking 'like crème brûlée'. This poem never made publication on account of a mentor vehemently disputing the crème brûlée image. I was reluctantly persuaded that water is not, and cannot be, the same as a set custard.

few days sleeping, reading, swimming and eating in the resort restaurant. I didn't feel able to venture outside of the grounds; I was nagged by the feeling of 'wasting' the trip. I was nagged by the feeling I'd caused myself harm – financial, emotional harm.

For the last two nights I booked the only five-star hotel on the island. Here I fought against competing desires to stay in bed, to punish myself for being so excessive, to play at being rich. I had a beautiful marble bathroom and I would bathe then shower then swim but all the while I felt this curtailment of pleasure – everything was a bit off.

On my last day I swam to the underwater ledge at the lip of a shell-shaped pool and curled myself up there as though against someone else's body. I wanted to cry. I tried to cry. I knew if it came it would be a kind of climax, my body would lurch in ways I was not in control of. I did not cry. The pool was empty, dark as a lake in shade. I had one of those moments of bold thought that you feel might change you forever: I would never be loved in the body I am in by someone I could trust with it. I had never felt loved in the body I am in. How could I enjoy a shell-shaped pool when I didn't know if I would ever feel loved? I was desiccating from the lack of it.

I arrived back in England and spent the next two weeks in bed recovering from flu. People asked about my holiday. I reported the bodies of water I'd floated in and the meals I'd eaten.

I'd failed at my task. I was tired, overspent. Instead of the stability I craved I had an aching doubtfulness about what next; my emotional ground felt danger-ously uneven. I was unable to perceive my life beyond the party I'd planned to celebrate my birthday. I combined the party with the launch of my book of poems. This had a mildly displacing effect and made me feel more entitled to demand people celebrate me. Even so, I was so fearful of having a breakdown after the party that I booked in some days off to allow for whatever might follow.

The party was glorious. Friends brought along a cake iced with the title of my book. Friends wore their hottest, flashiest clothes. My siblings danced with me to the music from our childhood car journeys. My name was spelled out in gold foil balloons on the stage. My mum sat on my sofa when I brought the party back to my flat, her eyes sober and amused as we did karaoke. If nothing else, I'd done the party right.

And then I was alone and the carnival was over.

London was in a heatwave. The Monday following the party I decided I would drive to the Ladies' Pond. I wanted fresh water. I stopped at a bakery and bought a sandwich and then slowly travelled up to north London. I had a keen awareness of moving towards my past, the risk of being confronted by the loveliness of the young adult me. Kentish Town Road, Highgate Hill, Parliament Hill Fields. These remain potent landmarks of something I can see but no longer access. It took me a long time to find somewhere to park. I was stressed by this point and struck again by a feeling that I have the right plans, but somehow conduct myself in a way that cancels out the pleasure I am seeking. It would have been better not to drive.

I wandered down through Highgate to the Pond. I was already wearing my swimsuit. As soon as I arrived I found a dry spot to stash my bag, took my clothes off and since there was a long queue for the ladder into the water, jumped straight in.

I hadn't timed my breathing well. I came back up to the surface snorting out water and coughing, my lungs pondy. As my breathing returned to normal I told myself to take notice: the lush minerality of the water, the tender weediness I swam toward, the ducklings skirting the edge. The Pond was full but I was alone in my sensations, paying attention to what being in the Pond activated within me. This was pleasure.

When I felt ready to get out, when a swim-hunger had settled in me like a cat growing heavier on my lap, I found a towel-shaped strip on the crowded grass behind the Pond. I sat and ate my sandwich* and drank a lukewarm fizzy drink. The women around me, mainly in pairs or groups, seemed to communicate a subtle joyfulness. I could be alone, but I was somehow also protected by this gathering, this aura of desire being met.

As I prepared to leave, I watched as a family of ducklings climbed over the back legs of a woman who was sunbathing next to me. The ducks literally walked all over her. They knew she would give safe passage to the water.

---

* I thought I'd bought a prosciutto sandwich but it turned out to be roasted red pepper. I am not enthusiastic about peppers and I picked the sandwich apart in the hope I'd discover some ham. It had become very warm and the oil from the peppers had soaked into the bread. I ate it, I had that post-swim hunger, but my brain was committed to the idea of it being a prosciutto sandwich and each bite somehow confused me, as though I was eating an apple disguised as a potato.

The First

AVA WONG DAVIES

I haven't been swimming in a long time – not since school, when I was on the swimming team. It was a big deal – the only sport I was vaguely competent at – but in the last four years I've drifted away from it, become more internal, not so unquestioningly physical and comfortable in my body.

(When I was little my mum called me a water baby because I loved taking baths. Still do.)

I slip out of bed at 5 a.m. one morning in late June, fan whirring huskily in the corner of the room, and I pad down to the bus stop at the top of my road. The morning is dove-grey, sunlight pressing through a light layer of cloud. Eighty-six minutes to get to the Pond, Citymapper notifies me. I need to take the 27, then the 214, then walk for fifteen minutes. I could get the Tube – it would be faster – but I like seeing the city undulate out of the window. I doze in my seat. West London sits hazy. It'll be scalding today.

(I went through a break-up recently. We were together for two years. It's alien to wake up and not hear him breathing next to me.)

I'm glad it's not sunny this morning. Walking down the hill from the bus stop to the entrance of the Heath, I can see pale light edging out of the greenery. I half run down the slope and feel my muscles loosening, warming.

(I feel like I'm walking around with this big stone of sad at the bottom of my ribcage and I don't know how to make it dissolve.)

I asked Jen if she wanted to come with me a few days ago, and she squealed with delight. She lives in Hackney, and I think about our paths through the city arcing upwards and finally converging at this one point. Except – Jen's lost. She's somewhere on the Heath, wandering the moors, picking her way through the heather and brambles. I try to call her but the reception is terrible. We find each other eventually and hug, heavy-lidded, smiling sillily. We follow a pair of older women, wiry and strong, making their way down a dirt path, totes slung over their shoulders.

(I've found it hard recently to look at myself in full length mirrors.)

We find a dark bench at the side of one of the meadows and slip off leggings and socks, stuffing them into our bags, leaving them free and open. Jen whispers to me, asks if our stuff will be safe. I say yes instinctively. I place my towel neatly beside my bag and look down at myself. I feel like my swimming costume is too revealing – like it betrays me as not a proper Pond swimmer. It's white and black, with a plunging neckline, and by the end of the summer the white will have stained a permanent, dusty cream, and my friends will grimace when I pull it out of my bag. Eventually, I will throw it out and replace it with a basic black Speedo. I adjust the crotch surreptitiously, cross an arm over my belly.

(I can't bear this new self-consciousness around my body, but it's been thrown into relief since that relationship ended. I feel far more aware of how it moves, of every curve and slope. It's been a long time since my body has been fully my own and I know I have to reckon with it now. I have so much unlearning to do.)

We're cautious and ease ourselves into the water ('we'll dive next time,' we say) and I'm reminded of swimming in the Irish Sea as a five year old, the massive pebbles on Greystones beach and my dad, younger, more tanned, smiling and scooping me up onto his shoulders. I think I like to romanticise things.

(I almost did something very rash last night but my friends convinced me otherwise. I think I was excited about going to the Pond – am excited about being at the Pond – but I also think there is a kernel of that thing still buried inside my chest somewhere.)

As I push off into the wetness I disturb a tiny fuzzy duckling who's paddling rapidly after its mother. I apologise and then feel ridiculous. I can feel my body starting to work in a way that it doesn't normally. I slip back into a rhythm I haven't actively participated in since I was sixteen.

Push out, pull back, kick, glide.

Keep it streamlined. Don't flail around underwater. Keep your toes pointed, fingers together. Swim like a shark.

(The pool we used for the swimming team was always a little too warm, a little too chlorinated. It made your teeth feel fuzzy and your hair crusty.)

There are a few other women here, but not many. They're solitary, quiet, purposeful. The heron stands sentinel on a buoy at the far end of the Pond. We swim towards it. The water feels clean, glassy.

I don't think about anything aside from the water on my skin.

Jen and I tread water for a while, chatting, laughing, receiving raised eyebrows from the more serious swimmers in flowery caps. After a while, I dip my head before

I rise up and shake my hair out. I enjoy the way my body moves.

We do a few laps before getting out but I could stay in the water for hours. I feel peaceful in a way that I haven't for a long time. I want to come back here with friends on hot, sunny days, but I also want to come back on my own and swim in the rain, be the only one in the water.

Jen goes to work, and I go home. I nap lazily in the heat, ignoring the pre-wedding hum in the flat. My brother is getting married on the weekend and my family are arriving from Malaysia. I can hear them rumbling in the hallway, shouting non-specifically. I dream about mud rising between my toes and weeds wrapping around my ankles. When I shower properly, later on, I find specks of silt in my cleavage.

(I can still feel the stone in my chest but I think it's OK that it's there.)

Like a Rat

ELI GOLDSTONE

I answered an ad on Gumtree for a room in an attic in Hampstead, a self-contained flat in the rafters of a house belonging to an elderly psychologist who seemingly had no idea how much rent she could have been charging. It was completely wood panelled and the back wall consisted of an enormous sliding window. There was a view out over the Heath. There was a kitchenette with a toaster oven and a sink. The bathroom had only a bath, which I found very romantic. It was heated by a single electric radiator. I didn't have quite enough money but the room was such a great deal that I felt - spiritually - obliged to take it. I moved in and I took on extra modelling work wherever I could get it - at fine art schools and drop-in classes in cold rooms above pubs, as well as privately for painters. According to my landlady, nobody else had responded to the advert. So, I suppose, she was stuck with me. She didn't care about my life, my habits or my personality. I fantasised about us becoming friends, but she resolutely would *not* facilitate it. I occasionally fed her cat when she went away, which meant I could pick through her books and finger every greasy object in her kitchen. The cat's bowl was absolutely revolting, caked in stale meat that in the summer contained bloated grains of rice that were – on closer inspection – maggots. I resolutely believe that all landlords are evil and that this person was the single exception to that rule. Her name was Phyllis.

I didn't have much of a social life because I didn't have the wherewithal to maintain close friendships. I spent my time mostly with the people I was sleeping with or modelled for – sometimes both. I found myself around a group of strange old-money relics who skied and bitched boringly about one another's oil paintings and competed to get me into bed. I learned that there were certain colleges of Oxford that were more acceptable than others, and that being 'chippy' was absolutely the worst thing that you could be described as, unluckily for me. At that point I felt I was rehearsing for a life that was owed to me. I thought of myself as a rich person trapped in a poor person's body.

At night I walked my dog, breathing in the smell of other people's clean laundry. I heard pianos being played and I peered in at laid tables and I dreamt my wet dreams of money.

I cooked stupid, elaborate meals for people. I made a coq au Riesling with a twenty-five pound bottle of Riesling for a man whose name I can't even remember . . . When I had no company, I ate like a rat. After dark I stole from the bins of a local patisserie. I ate huge loaves of dry bread made with beautiful olive oil, cream from the inside of stale choux buns and smashed-up chocolate gateaux. I was hungry – I spent eight hours of the day contorted while various people pointed at my body and named parts of it. *Scapula*, *dimples of Venus*, etc. I loved having so much attention paid to my body, which I considered to be pretty extraordinary. I showed it to people in my spare time as well as to make money. I slept with people who lived lives I found interesting and whose worlds I felt I was allowed limited access to. But we never went anywhere! I had no more access to these things than before.

I got knocked up. The guy in question was a Classics graduate, whatever that is . . . He would whisper to me in High German in public, as a sort of foreplay. It was excruciating. When I texted him about my pregnancy, he replied, *Are you sure it's mine?* And I replied, *Are you fucking serious?*

As summer began, I swam in the Ladies' Pond. When I was too hungover or lazy to swim I lay on the grass, considering the possibility of swimming. I liked the smell of my skin afterwards - soupy and menstrual. I was used to being the only nude body in a room full of clothed ones, or in front of a singular man. I was used to being scrutinised, assessed, moved, interpreted. It was so nice to be naked in the company of other women. It was so nice not to be looked at. One morning at the Pond I caught sight of a girl I had kissed. She was lying with her friends. She had a string bikini top on and her arms were crossed over her forehead to protect her eyes from the glare of the sun. She had a soft, brown moustache. I found her intensely sexy. Instead of trying to draw her attention, I packed my book into my bag and left. I felt that my desire towards her was urgent and intrusive. I was jealous, too, of how she looked.

The crowds started to bother me as the summer worked itself up. At some point it occurred to me that I could break in and swim in the Pond in the middle of the night if I wanted to. After a certain time the Heath was empty of everyone except perverts like me. It was the first time I'd experienced a really, absolutely dark place in the city. I liked to have it all to myself, to walk alone and with purpose through the middle of it. I swam naked in the early hours of the morning.

I cut my feet kicking them against the rocks. One day friends came to visit and we lay on the brownish grass drinking cans and smoking and getting sunburnt until late. I told them about my nocturnal swims and they said, *Oh, we have to do that.* They looked at each other. *Can we do that?* Even people who prefer to obey the law can be persuaded to do a little breaking and entering. All you have to do is believe for a second that there is nothing that doesn't belong to you. It's so exhilarating to scramble and drop into a dark place like a penny!

The water made the breath stick in our chests and we laughed and shouted, slightly hysterical. Moonlight caught on each ripple that we made with our bodies. I felt so good about what was happening. I felt like a person capable of experiencing great pleasures. I feel like this occasionally, and at other times I feel like a person only capable of experiencing enormous pain. After a while of pacing back and forth on the water's edge nervously, my dog started to bark in alarm. We were too far from him and getting further away – he didn't understand what we were doing. He has always been afraid of water, and of being by himself. His barking was loud and insistent and high-pitched. The police arrived and waved torches around. I suppose my dog had snitched on us. They asked our names and addresses and we gave fake ones. I wish I could remember the pseudonyms we gave. I'm certain they were all very witty. I tried to control my impulse to get myself arrested. At times like that, faced with authority, I am the truest version of myself: horrid, self-righteous and feral. After we made our escape we were exhilarated. We walked to the pub for last orders. I had taken off my bra and carried it as a trophy, its cups heavy with pond water. We sat and drank whisky, our hair dripping onto the table and our voices as loud as we could get them.

My abortion was scheduled for the same day that my friend Jessica and I were hosting a fundraising party for a poetry magazine we had started. There were readings and I mixed gin cocktails. I wore a backless dress and underneath it a pair of hospital-issued disposable knickers. I was tired. There aren't many photos of the evening, but in one I am leaning on my decoupaged IKEA dining table, watching a stranger read out a poem, and I look tired.

My neighbours at the time were a couple who liked to have elaborate breakfasts on the balcony, which my room overlooked. I saw them spread their broadsheets over the table and drink fresh orange juice day after day. I wasn't jealous of their situation, which seemed too neat or something to be appealing. But they would catch my eye while I was smoking out of the window. They would make passive-aggressive comments about my dog's barking. I'm sure they spied on me. One late afternoon in August I was letting myself into the house when one of them caught me by the elbow and insisted on speaking to me. *Are you OK?* he asked. *You look dizzy.* I was caught off guard. Why would I be dizzy? *I'm fine*, I said. *Thank you.* He looked at me. *You know,* he said, *we're right next door. If you ever need anything. If there's anything we can do.* I still think about that . . . what it was they thought they could have done for me.

Nothing Much Except Joy

DEBORAH MOGGACH

I've been swimming in the Ladies' Pond for nearly half a century. In the early days, when I was a young mother living nearby, it was a godsend. I was engulfed in domesticity with two small children and struggling to write. I don't think I coped that well; one day a journalist came to my house and, in the resulting inter-view, mentioned 'the legendary Moggach chaos'. Only then did I realise the extent to which things had got out of control (and they didn't notice that the cat had defecated in a saucepan). That pond saved my sanity. Just now and then, when I could snatch a moment, I would grab my bike and pedal furiously to Hampstead Heath for a stolen half-hour of heaven.

Now I'm seventy, and the Ladies' Pond has truly been one of the wonders of my life. Slipping into its waters is slipping into bliss. It's a miracle that it still exists, open for everyone, in the middle of London; wherever you are in the world you know it's there, summer and winter, waiting for you. How sustaining that image is! When everything else around us is altering so quickly this is the most profound solace. The outside world is still there, of course. You can hear, through the trees, the rumble of mechanical diggers as yet another gargantuan mansion is built for some oligarch; you can watch a plane carrying poor sods to some business meeting, but the plane is far above you, glinting in the sun, as you serenely swim, the reeds brushing your toes while, in the trees, a kingfisher darts past in a flash of such brilliance it stops your breath.

Once you're in the water you're accepted by nature. You're in it, and part of it. My children love Parliament Hill Lido, and I'm sure they're right, but it's an artificial construct, a beautiful swimming pool. In the Ladies' Pond you're on nodding acquaintance with the wildlife. I remember swimming past a nest and watching a coot bearing a gift in its beak – a leaf or something equally pathetic. Its mate was sitting on her eggs. As he offered it to her, the look on her face was one that women everywhere would recognise: 'Er, thanks so much, hmm, it's just what I wanted . . .' The strained politeness on her face made me laugh out loud.

When I tell people I love swimming in the Ladies' Pond there are two reactions. The first: 'Ugh, isn't it muddy/dangerous/cold?' The other is, 'How wonderful, lucky old you.' Needless to say, the people I like best are the second lot. And I like the look of the other women who swim there too – free spirits, all of them – though I never talk to anybody. Swimming is a solitary activity; it's where I slip into a dream state and think up my plots. After a couple of circuits something loosens in my brain and I start making unusual connections. Writing is all about relationships – between sentences, between people, between changes of tone – and being submerged in another element can shake these around in a new formation.

In my fifties I moved to a house overlooking Hampstead Heath and for ten enchanted years lived a *rus in urbe* life. I had a dog, and kept chickens. I also had an allotment in Fitzroy Park, near the Ladies' Pond. I'd scavenge on the Heath for wood for the fire and hay for the hens. During the summer, and into the autumn, I'd work on my allotment and bike home, stopping at the Pond for a swim. Once or twice I climbed over the fence at night and swam in the moonlit water, the bats swooping around me. I don't think you can do that now – the gates are too high – but I remember it as utterly magical.

My house was nearer to the Mixed Pond and sometimes I'd swim there. I love it in a different way: its water is always a degree warmer and its lifeguards are more chatty. At the far end the water almost boils with giant carp, their lips gaping open like sex dolls. There's often a heron, and in summer a solitary tern swoops down to fish, having flown all the way from the Arctic.

And the atmosphere's different with men around. Noisier, certainly – why do men splutter and grunt like walruses when they swim, and splash water everywhere even when they're doing the crawl? And why does anyone do butterfly stroke, for goodness sake? It's always men, and they drench one's hair. But mixing the sexes can give a certain zip to things. I like watching boys showing off, leaping in with their arms around their knees – look at me, I'm all testosterone! – and girls squealing when they climb into the water. Then the flirtations as couples meet, clinging to a life ring, sleek as seals with their laughter ringing out. I especially like swimming at the Mixed Pond when the fairground's visiting and the whoops and screams and music float through the trees as one serenely paddles up and down.

Paddling's the word. I love to do it, but I'm not a stylish swimmer. I swim a vaguely lopsided breast-stroke, my head sticking up like a periscope to keep my hair dry. I can't do any other strokes, I can't dive and I'm not particularly tough, either. I'm on the lowest rungs of the pond hierarchy because I'm a fair-weather visitor, swimming from June to October. I gaze with admiration at those superior creatures who brave the water all year round, breaking the ice in the winter and generally making the rest of us feel like wimps. They know the lifeguards. They're tough. Many of these women are of a certain age and I'm sure they have impeccable left-wing credentials – this is Hampstead, after all, though the area has changed out of all recognition. It's filled with bankers now, braying estate agents with hangovers and hair gel, and 4x4s driven by trophy wives in leather trousers clogging up the streets on the school run. The old inhabitants – arty, messy, obstreperous – have mostly gone.

But you can still find them at the Ladies' Pond. I glimpse their wrinkled bodies when they strip naked in the changing room and realise, with a jolt, that I'm wrinkled too. I've joined them. I might not have joined their club, being too cowardly to break the ice, in every respect. But I join them in celebrating the camaraderie of the Ladies' Pond, and hope that a new generation is arriving to take their place.

Because there's something wild and anarchic about the Pond. It may be managed by the Corporation of London, but it remains a place of wildness and freedom, a beautiful sanctuary, and that's very precious. One day, when they're older, I hope to take my granddaughters there.

Autumn

Laundry

LEANNE SHAPTON

London, 2010. At eight a.m. I set out from the house, toward the Hampstead Heath Ladies' Pond. I can see my breath as I wend my way up the overgrown front path; I exhale long and slow to watch it as I cross the road and walk past a couple of magpies. One for sorrow, two for joy. On my right, the Long Pond is dark and green, then, over a hill and around a bend, the Mixed Pond grayish-brown on my left. I can feel the cold air through my sweater. September.

Three people are unfolding tables near a van in preparation for a marathon. In a wooded path two joggers pass, smelling of shampoo and laundry, lemony. The path dips and I hear women's laughter, its pitch distinctive. Voices carry crisp and dense over water, heads held high and tipped back to speak. The effort makes for breathy, cheerful barking. I can't see the Ladies' Pond, but I can hear it.

The pond water temperature, neatly written on a blackboard, is fourteen degrees Celsius. Two women circle the life preservers at the far end. Another swims steadily out toward a lily-padded patch. Two more stroke toward the concrete dock, one in a yellow cap. A few ducks and a pair of swans bob in the corner.

I know I have to get in without hesitating, one smooth movement from the top of the ladder into the murk. I slip in until my shoulders are submerged – the water stings and my breath balls in my throat, high and shallow. I can see only a few inches of my body before it dissolves into the olive dark.

I swim, moving every limb exaggeratedly to generate heat, then push face down to the farthest life preserver, toward the two women. When I get there I raise my head. One woman talks about how her child is adjusting to school. The other makes noises of assent and sympathy. I wonder: Did they come here as friends or befriend each other in the pond? How long have they been swimming in water this cold? Will I ever have a friend who swims in freezing ponds with me? I circle again and my body feels warm, but it is the warmth of a slap: blood rushing the flesh. Looking back toward the dock, I see another woman, wearing a black tank and a white cap, step calmly down the ladder.

After another turn I get out and wrap myself in the fluffy grey bath towel I grabbed from the bathroom of the house where I'm renting a room. My breath is still tight in my chest. The towel smells lemony too.

The unnaturally sweet laundry smell is a match scraped against deep feelings of longing. I'm obsessed with this smell. A detergent-fragrant scarf bought on eBay arrives in the mail and I debate whether to write the seller and ask what brand she washed it in. I buy unscented soap for my dermatitic skin, can't quite bring myself to buy dryer sheets, but part of me still wants my life to be suburb-scented.

When I was little, our family laundry was done with no-name detergent and line-dried until well into November. It didn't smell like anything to me. Now when I visit my parents' home and press my face into a towel, I smell my family. My mother's Filipino homemaking and my father's citrus-scrub mechanic's hand cleaner. The smell is mildly tarpaulin, with notes of canvas, bamboo, and limonene. Comforting, but harsh.

Edmonton, Alberta, 1987. I wake in the middle of the night, and by the colour of the darkness and the sound of an aquarium I know I'm not at home. I blink, lie very still, and remember: Jen, Stephanie, and I are being billeted in the basement of somebody's Edmonton home. I am lying on my side on a pullout couch; my two sleeping teammates are in the room, Jen on a couch across from me, Stephanie on a mattress on the floor.

It is warm in my Miss Piggy sleeping bag – we are all in sleeping bags – and smells like the inside of a van. My mother made a liner, two striped twin-bedsheets sewn together, and I'm twisted inside them, beneath Miss Piggy's giant lashed eyes, her mouth slightly open in a happy Muppety expression. The clock on my new yellow stopwatch, wound around my wrist, reads 4:15 a.m.

I close my eyes and try to sleep again, but I'm thinking of hotel rooms, the comforting sterile non-smell, the hum of ice machines. I'm thinking of breakfast upstairs in the kitchen of this house in a few hours, of demonstrating table manners, the strange swimmers from the other team whose house this is, their non-swimming siblings, cheerful chatter, and the selection of breakfast cereal. I always wind up eating too much or too little in other people's houses. I hope the billeting mother will not make eggs.

Turning over onto my back I can dimly see a few things on the panelled walls: a poster of Corey Hart, another of a baseball team, a framed landscape. I close my eyes. The meet starts tomorrow. We drove straight to the Edmonton pool from the airport, lugging our bags through the locker rooms and onto the deck. It was an easy practice. I used a yellow kickboard that belonged to a swimmer from the University of Calgary team, the Dinos, and I wanted to steal it.

I decide to do my race. I turn onto my stomach, tuck my head into the sleeping bag and begin. My stopwatch beeps and wakes Stephanie.

'What the—?'

Before every race I'd rub my hands on the top of the block to make them raw and more sensitive in the water. I'd know the push, the ripping sound of entry, the silence, the gauging of depth, and the repetitive, urging noises when my head broke the surface of the water. I could always recognize my coach's voice in the crowd. (The images, the intense anticipation and strain I'd conjure in bed, would be replaced, a decade later, with the men I'd imagine sleeping with.)

As I touch and turn for the last length, hackneyed expressions like *pour it on*, *flat out*, *mad dash*, *closing in* spool in my head. Suddenly the yellow Omega touchpad. I click down hard on my stopwatch: the blue digits read 1:12:07.

The sound of the aquarium.

'Fucking enough with the beeping and panting already. It's like four in the morning.'

Stephanie, from the mattress on the floor.

I stand for a few chilly minutes and watch the pond. Two women get out, another gets in. I gather my things. In the shedlike locker room I watch what the other women do, and imitate them. They strip down and rinse the pond water from their suits and bodies. Standing under a lukewarm shower I eavesdrop. One woman swears by her partial wetsuit, another swims through to December. Something about a school, about a woman they all know, about someone else's handbag. We face the walls as we change, our skin white and red. As I head back across the Heath I wave to the guards, the damp towel wrapped double around my neck and over my nose so I can walk along breathing in its smell, now mixed with a greenish whiff of duckweed.

A Quietening

SOPHIE MACKINTOSH

There are years that hum like an electric charge; there are years steady with peace. Cold winter gives way to spring, and within me fear and hope jostle for space. London becomes a battleground for quiet, but how can you find quiet when the commotion is inside your own head?

At the heart of everything is my phone, comforter and enabler. I try out measures, such as leaving the phone in the bedroom when I am watching television or reading, but soon invent excuses and end up lying over the bed, scrolling in the old familiar pattern. Or I leave it at home when I go to the shops, returning only to binge – a compulsive, shameful itch. And before I scratch it, the heady feeling of not having checked for forty minutes, the possibilities contained within that untethered time.

I start to seek out activities that require me to leave my phone behind, unchecked. I want to break the cycle.

In April we take a trip to the Heath and try our first swim of the year. It is the Mixed Pond, which I've never been to before. Though the weather is unseasonably hot, the water is far too cold for me, and I remember too late that water temperatures are a kind of trick – twelve degrees centigrade means something different than it does with air, icier. But I go in regardless and as I tread water, breathlessly, I remember all the things I have learned about cold water shock, about the conspiracy it plays on your body. About the importance of acclimatisation. The lifeguard watches me flounder until I get the hint and climb out, looking on as my partner and his best friend swim off.

The journey back to my towel is a walk of shame. I do not like the Mixed Pond, with its scrubby strip of grass and groups of people watching as you stumble past, goosepimpled, in a bikini. Under those circumstances, pushed up close with everyone, sitting on a patch of dirt, my frantic thoughts don't stop. I miss the topography of the Ladies' Pond, the calmness, the water that would surely not expel me with such indignity.

In May I take a week off work, but I still check my email so much that the battery can drain within two hours. The Ladies' Pond then becomes a sort of sanctuary, because being on your phone is frowned upon. I go there on my second day off, and abide by the rules; I don't check my phone at all. Still wary of the cold water, I lie in the meadow and read my book. The city feels like a dream, a hundred miles away, clean air and grass against my cheek.

Sometimes it feels like London will chew you up but also put you back together. There's a deep unfairness to it, I think sometimes – resentful at how drained I am, at the bad decisions the late-night splendour of the city enables me to make – and how all it takes is one summertime walk through a place like the Heath to make me forgive and forget. In the Pond everything fades away: expensive taxis, corner-shop wine purchased at 3 a.m., taking the tube in the morning dressed in last night's clothes while swigging from a bottle of water. There is no better hangover cure, me and my friends agree. No better forgiveness. No better permission to be still.

There was a time, not so long ago, when I wasn't addicted to my phone. When I first moved to London I didn't have a smartphone and I drew maps to job

interviews on my forearms and the backs of my hands.
I could not tweet ill-advised things from house parties
or take artful photographs to post on Instagram. All I
could do was text and call; my battery lasted for three
days at a time. My phone was not a comfort blanket
but purely functional.

Now I wonder how I lived without it as I navi-
gate my way to the Pond. Though I've been there so
many times I have a strange blind spot about reaching
the Ladies' Pond, as if it's a pool from myth or fairy-
tale that switches its location. This effect is enhanced
by the swerving of the 4G, the unreliable blip of
my Google Maps app, sending me deeper into the
heart of the green space when I should be hugging
the edges. I've accepted now that I just need to let
instinct guide where I'm going, to put my phone into
my bag and trust that I will get there, even when
leaves or trees make the route feel unfamiliar, even
when not having my phone in my hand feels like a
physical, unbearable discomfort.

Summer draws on; the water becomes warmer, and
my life becomes different. I swim then, alone or with
friends, dipping my body through the silky murk. I am
performative about my swimming, so that the lifeguards
believe I won't drown. I am always having to prove

things to myself and want to be graceful, but nothing I do is cohesive or neat – not swimming, not writing. Everything can feel so overwhelming, except for when I am here, uncontactable whether I like it or not. When a dragonfly flies past my head my first instinct is to take a photo, but of course I am submerged.

One of my favourite parts of the Ladies' Pond in summer is getting out. Lying on your towel, no need to dry yourself, just waiting for the scorching air to make the water a memory. All around you are bodies packed into the available space but never as intrusively as at the Mixed Pond, women having grown up with the awareness of the space we take up, women wanting to give room to women. It is these women I defer to when I fight against the instinct to look at my phone. I am saying to the world: you can wait.

Still, sometimes in summer the meadow is full of groups of friends and you are alone, trying to find a patch of grass for your towel, and the air feels too febrile and heavy with gossip and tempers fray in the heat. Sometimes I like to be one body in a sea of bodies, but mostly my heart jumps upon seeing plenty of room in the meadow. This is why autumn is my favourite season for the Pond. It's a slip of time very easy to miss – the end of summer giving way to crispness, yet still just hot enough to swim and be outside. It's a space of a couple of weeks, at most. Every visit during this time feels elegiac, and like you're getting away with something, extending the season secretly and lavishly. Sun on your skin, the water cool but not yet unbearable.

Autumn is the most wholesome time of year in London; the back-to-school feeling, the perfect light, the sense of the year's close drawing nearer and compelling you to take stock and catch your breath. To walk through the green of the Heath and to the place where all is calm, still, where the meadow is empty except for a few women like you reading a book, making the most of the last sunlight. It is a peace that fills something in me.

Autumn this year means a quietening. The frenzied anxiety of the summer gives way to space, finally, something more contemplative. On my last visit to the Pond, I know it is probably my final swim of the year, so I make it count. I stay in the water for as long as possible, and then with all the blood rushing along my limbs I walk to a pub for a pint and a pork pie, a long read of a book, phone mostly tucked away.

The idea that wholesomeness does not have to be a thing snatched in gulps is something that is occurring to me more and more. That the Pond will be there for me next summer, whatever that brings, whatever my life looks like then.

About the Contributors

Ava Wong Davies is a freelance theatre critic and playwright based in London. She won the Harold Hobson Sunday Times Award for theatre criticism in 2018. She writes regularly for *Exeunt Magazine* and *The Stage*, and has written arts criticism for *The Line of Best Fit*, *Fest Magazine*, *Girls on Tops* and the *Independent*, as well as on avawongdavies.wordpress.com. She is currently part of the Soho Theatre Writers Lab 2018–19.

Margaret Drabble was born in Sheffield in 1939 and was educated at Newnham College, Cambridge. She is the author of nineteen novels including *A Summer Bird-Cage*, *The Millstone*, *The Peppered Moth*, *The Red Queen*, *The Sea Lady*, *The Pure Gold Baby* and, most recently,

The Dark Flood Rises. She has also written biographies, screenplays and was the editor of the *Oxford Companion to English Literature*. She was appointed CBE in 1980 and made DBE in the 2008 Honours list. She was also awarded the 2011 Golden PEN Award for a Lifetime's Distinguished Service to Literature. She is married to the biographer Michael Holroyd.

Esther Freud was born in London in 1963. As a young child she travelled through Morocco with her mother and sister, returning to England aged six where she attended a Rudolf Steiner school in Sussex. In 1979 she moved to London to study Drama, going on to work as an actress, mostly in the theatre. Her first novel, *Hideous Kinky*, was published in 1992 and was shortlisted for the John Llewellyn Rhys Prize and made into a film. In 1993, after the publication of her second novel, *Peerless Flats*, she was named by Granta as one of the Best of Young British Novelists under 40. She has since written seven novels, including *The Sea House*, *Love Falls*, *Lucky Break* and most recently *Mr Mac & Me*. Her first play, *Stitchers*, played to sold out houses at Jermyn St Theatre in June 2018. She also writes stories, articles and travel pieces for newspapers and magazines, and teaches creative writing, in her own local group and at the Faber Academy. She lives between London and Suffolk.

Nell Frizzell is a freelance writer and casual lifeguard. She has written for, among others, the *Guardian*, *VICE*, the *Telegraph*, *Elle*, *Grazia*, the *Observer* and is a *Vogue* columnist. She spent two happy summers standing on the deck of the Kenwood Ladies' Pond as a lifeguard. Nell has also featured several times on BBC Radio 4's Woman's Hour, Short Cuts and as a guest on Radio 5 Live, BBC London and (surprisingly often) on BBC Radio Ulster. As well as journalism, Nell has written and performed comedy, is a seamstress and knitter, and spends an inordinate amount of time trying to teach her baby to love the outdoors as much as she does.

Eli Goldstone is a writer born in Manchester and based in Margate. Her first novel, *Strange Heart Beating*, was published by Granta in 2017 and in 2018 won a Betty Trask Award. She is an alumna of the Creative Writing (Novels) MA at City University, London and the previous prose editor of *Cadaverine*.

Amy Key's second poetry collection, *Isn't Forever*, a Poetry Book Society Wild Card Choice, was published by Bloodaxe in June 2018 and was named a book of the year in the *Guardian*, *The Times* and the *Irish Times*. Her poems have been widely published in magazines including *Granta*, *The White Review*, *Poetry*, *The Poetry Review*, *Poetry London* and *Broadly*, and in anthologies from Faber & Faber, Penguin and Ignota Books. She is currently writing a hybrid work of creative non-fiction and poetry.

Jessica J. Lee is a British-Canadian-Taiwanese author and environmental historian. Her first book, *Turning: A Swimming Memoir*, was published by Virago in 2017 and named among the best books of the year by both Canadian newspaper *the National Post* and German newspaper *Die Zeit*. She has a PhD in Environmental History and Aesthetics and completed her dissertation on the history of Hampstead Heath. She was Writer-in-Residence at the Leibniz Institute for Freshwater Ecology in Berlin from 2017–2018 and has written for BBC Radio 4, *TLS* and *MUNCHIES*, among others. Her second book, *Two Trees Make a Forest: A story of memory, migration, and Taiwan*, will be published in 2019 by Virago. Jessica lives in Berlin.

Sophie Mackintosh was born in South Wales in 1988, and is currently based in London. Her fiction, essays and poetry have been published by *Granta*, *The White Review*, the *New York Times* and *The Stinging Fly*, among others. Her short story 'Grace' was the winner of the 2016 White Review Short Story Prize, and her story 'The Running Ones' won the Virago/Stylist Short Story competition in 2016. Sophie's debut novel *The Water Cure* was published in 2018 and was longlisted for the Man Booker Prize. Her second novel *Blue Ticket* will be published in 2020.

So Mayer is a writer, bookseller, and activist. Their recent projects are collaborative essay *Tender Questions* (with Preti Taneja, Peninsula Press, 2019), the TinyLetter Disturbing Words, and poetry chapbook *<jacked a kaddish>* (Litmus Publishing, 2019), as well as the introduction for *Spells: 21st Century Occult Poetry* (eds. Sarah Shin and Rebecca Tamás, Ignota Books, 2019). Previous work includes *Political Animals: New Feminist Cinema* (IB Tauris, 2015) and *(O)* (Arc, 2015), and a decade of writing on film culture for *Sight & Sound*, *The F-Word* and *Literal Magazine*. So works at Burley Fisher Books and with queer feminist film curators, Club des Femmes, and is a co-founder of Raising Films.

Deborah Moggach was born in 1948. She is the author of eighteen novels including the bestselling *Tulip Fever*. In 2012, her novel *These Foolish Things* was adapted for the screen under the title *The Best Exotic Marigold Hotel*. An award-winning screenwriter, she won a Writers' Guild Award for her adaptation of Anne Fine's *Goggle-Eyes* and her screenplay for the 2005 adaptation of *Pride and Prejudice* was nominated for a BAFTA. Deborah was appointed an OBE in the

2018 New Year's Honours List for services to literature and drama. She lives in Wales with her husband, Mark.

Nina Mingya Powles was born in New Zealand and partly grew up in China. She is the author of several poetry pamphlet collections, most recently *field notes on a downpour* (2018) and *Luminescent* (2017). Her poems and essays have been widely published in New Zealand, the US and the UK, including in *Poetry, Daikon, Hainamana Arts* and *The Willowherb Review*. In 2018 she was one of three winners of the inaugural Women Poets' Prize. She is poetry editor of *The Shanghai Literary Review* and founding editor of *Bitter Melon*, a new poetry pamphlet press. Her prose debut, a food memoir, will be published by The Emma Press in 2019.

Leanne Shapton is an artist, illustrator and writer who was born in Toronto and lives in New York. She is the author of several books, including *Swimming Studies, The Native Trees of Canada, Women in Clothes* (with Sheila Heti and Heidi Julavits), *Important Artifacts and Personal Property from the Collection of Lenore Doolan and Harold Morris* and *Guestbook: Ghost Stories*. She is the co-founder of J&L Books, a non-profit imprint specializing in photography.

Lou Stoppard was born in Luton in 1990 and currently lives in London. She is a writer and curator focusing on culture and style. Her writing has appeared in the *Financial Times*, *The New Yorker* and various international editions of *Vogue*. Her exhibitions have been staged at venues including Open Eye Gallery in Liverpool and Somerset House in London and cover themes such as the cultural influence of the North of England and fashion's approach to youth and teen-agehood. Her books include *Fashion Together: Fashion's Most Extraordinary Duos on the Art of Collaboration*, published in 2017.

Sharlene Teo was born in Singapore and lives in London. She is the winner of the inaugural Deborah Rogers Writer's Award. Her debut novel, *Ponti*, was shortlisted for the Hearst Big Book Award and the Edward Stanford Award for Fiction with a Sense of Place and selected by Ali Smith as one of the best debut works of fiction published in 2018.

A Further Note on the Pond and The Kenwood Ladies' Pond Association

Managed by The City of London Corporation since 1989, the Ladies' Pond is open throughout the year and monitored by lifeguards. Swimming times vary according to the season. All women and girls above the age of eight may swim at the Pond. Transgender women are welcome at the Pond.

Swimming through the winter is increasingly popular but it is important to acclimatise properly. It is recommended that you swim at least twice a week so that your body becomes used to the cold temperatures.

The Kenwood Ladies' Pond Association (KLPA) is an organisation run by an elected committee of volunteers. Its aim is to help preserve the Pond, which has been under threat of development in the past, as well as to foster a sense of community. Swimmers are welcome to become members.

Nicky Mayhew and Julia Dick were co-chairs of the KLPA during the period when this collection was conceived of and put together, and the Publishers wish to thank them for their assistance and support.

Permissions

The Publisher gratefully acknowledges permission to reproduce extracts from the following:

> Quote from *Waterlog* by Roger Deakin reproduced by permission of the Estate of Roger Deakin c/o Georgina Capel Associates Ltd., 29 Wardour Street, London W1D 6PS.

> Extract from U. A. Fanthorpe, 'Rising Damp', in *UAF New and Collected Poems* (Enitharmon, 2010).

> Quote from Rosemary Tonks, *Bedouin of the London Evening: Collected Poems & Selected Prose* (Bloodaxe Books, 2014), by permission of the publisher.

Daunt Books

Founded in 2010, the Daunt Books imprint is dedicated to discovering brilliant works by talented authors from around the world. Whether reissuing beautiful new editions of lost classics or introducing fresh literary voices, we're drawn to writing that evokes a strong sense of place – novels, short fiction, memoirs, travel accounts, and translations with a lingering atmosphere, a thrilling story, and a distinctive style. With our roots as a travel bookshop, the titles we publish are inspired by the Daunt shops themselves, and the exciting atmosphere of discovery to be found in a good bookshop.

For more information, please visit
www.dauntbookspublishing.co.uk

2019

Voices in the Evening | Natalia Ginzburg
With an introduction by Colm Tóibín
'Sharp and lively.' – Lydia Davis

The Solace of Open Spaces | Gretel Ehrlich
With an introduction by Amy Liptrot
'Vivid, tough, and funny. Wyoming has found its Whitman.'
– Annie Dillard

Aetherial Worlds | Tatyana Tolstaya
Translated by Anya Migdal
'Everything in this generous writer's hands is vivid and alive.'
– Joy Williams

Map of Another Town | M.F.K. Fisher
'She is not just a great food writer. She is a great writer, full stop.'
– Rachel Cooke, *Observer*

2018

Sherlock Holmes and the Adventure of the Blue Carbuncle
Arthur Conan Doyle
'The world's most famous detective.' – Ruth Rendell

Consider the Oyster | M.F.K. Fisher
Foreword by Felicity Cloake
'Her writing makes your mouth water.' – *Financial Times*

The Pine Barrens | John McPhee
Foreword by Iain Sinclair
'McPhee's genius is that he can write about anything.'
– Robert Macfarlane

Family Lexicon | Natalia Ginzburg
Introduction by Tim Parks | Translated by Jenny McPhee
'A masterpiece.' – *The New Yorker*

Cassandra at the Wedding | Dorothy Baker
'Witty and assured, dark but jaunty, off-handedly smart.'
– *London Review of Books*

In the Distance | Hernan Diaz
'A brutal, sad, tender coming-of-age story.' – *Guardian*

*Ants Among Elephants: An Untouchable Family and the Making
of Modern India* | Sujatha Gidla
'A vital and illuminating book.' – Arundhati Roy

The Little Virtues | Natalia Ginzburg
Introduction by Rachel Cusk | Translated by Dick Davis
'I really love and admire *The Little Virtues*.' – Zadie Smith

A Small Place | Jamaica Kincaid
'An unaffectedly sumptuous, irresistible writer.' – Susan Sontag

Tomorrow | Elisabeth Russell Taylor
Introduction by Alison Moore
'Haunting, beautifully written.' – *Financial Times*

2017

A Cat, a Man, and Two Women | Junichiro Tanizaki
'A tour de force – catnip.' – *New York Times*

Christmas with Dull People | Saki
'Saki was irreplaceable and unreplaced.'
– *London Review of Books*

The Nachman Stories | Leonard Michaels
Introduction by David Bezmozgis
'Superbly crafted and all too human.' – *The Sunday Times*

Pull Me Under | Kelly Luce
'A natural born writer.' – Rachel Kushner

Lillian Boxfish Takes a Walk | Kathleen Rooney
'Like taking a street-level tour through six decades
of New York.' – *New York Times*

The Gastronomical Me | M.F.K. Fisher
Introduction by Bee Wilson
'The greatest food writer who has ever lived.' – Simon Schama

Dark at the Crossing | Elliot Ackerman
'Hauntingly evocative and beautiful.' – Elif Shafak

The Crofter and the Laird | John McPhee
'A book full of such clear-sighted details and wildness.'
– *Sunday Times*

A Broken Mirror | Mercè Rodoreda
Translated by Josep Miquel Sobrer
'Rodoreda has bedazzled me.' – Gabriel García Marquez

2016

London Perceived | V.S. Pritchett
'Pritchett's essays are marvels.' – James Wood

The Trial of Lady Chatterley's Lover | Sybille Bedford
Introduction by Thomas Grant
'Absolutely superb.' – *A Good Read*, BBC Radio 4

Oranges | John McPhee
Foreword by Richard Mabey
'A classic of American reportage.' – Julian Barnes

The Men's Club | Leonard Michaels
'One of the best American stylists of the twentieth century.'
– David Bezmozgis

Villa Triste | Patrick Modiano
Translated by John Cullen
'A masterpiece of insidious intent.' – *Telegraph*

Ways to Disappear | Idra Novey
'Lush and tightly woven.' – *New York Times Book Review*

Marie | Madeleine Bourdouxhe
Translated by Faith Evans
'This existential classic might be the most French novel
I've ever read.' – Nicholas Lezard, *Guardian*

Ice-Candy Man | Bapsi Sidhwa
'Compulsively readable.' – *Observer*

Jack & Rochelle: A Holocaust Story of Love and Resistance
Jack and Rochelle Sutin | Edited by Laurence Sutin
'Powerful and illuminating.' – *New York Times Book Review*

Green On Blue | Elliot Ackerman
'Utterly absorbing.' – Khaled Hosseini

Light Box | K.J. Orr
'A distinctive new voice.' – Tessa Hadley

2015

His Monkey Wife | John Collier
'A wayward masterpiece.' – Anthony Burgess

One Point Two Billion | Mahesh Rao
'These stories are a deeply satisfying read.' – Kamila Shamsie

Fierce Attachments | Vivian Gornick
'A brilliant book, a classic of its kind.' – Rachel Cooke, *Observer*

Coming into the Country | John McPhee
Foreword by Robert Macfarlane
'A grand master of narrative non-fiction.' – *Guardian*

Sylvia | Leonard Michaels
Foreword by David Lodge
'Terrifying, beautiful and addictive.' – Ian McEwan

Peking Picnic | Ann Bridge
'Beautiful, grave, humorous, exciting, and wise.' – *Observer*

The Crow Eaters | Bapsi Sidhwa
'One of the great comic novels of the 20th century.'
– Hanif Kureishi

The Isle of Youth | Laura van den Berg
'Absolutely captivating.' – *Vanity Fair*

Dom Casmurro | Machado de Assis
Foreword by Elizabeth Hardwick | Translated by Helen Caldwell
'A work of breathtaking versatility.' – *TLS*

2014

Duveen | S. N. Behrman
'A masterful, deeply enjoyable work.'
– David Remnick, *The New Yorker*

La Femme de Gilles | Madeleine Bourdouxhe
Translated by Faith Evans
'A little masterpiece.' – *The Sunday Times*

Park Notes | Sarah Pickstone
'Beautifully crafted ruminations on Regent's Park.' – *Observer*

Pleasures and Landscapes: A Traveller's Tales From Europe
Sybille Bedford | Introduction by Jan Morris
'She cannot write a dull page.' – *Financial Times*

A Good Place to Die | James Buchan
'A must-read.' – Donna Leon

The Smoke is Rising | Mahesh Rao
'An exceptionally accomplished novel.' – Siddhartha Deb

Miss Lonelyhearts | Nathanael West
'A masterpiece.' – Jonathan Lethem

2013

The London Scene | Virginia Woolf
Introduction by Hermione Lee
'1930s London comes alive.' – *Washington Post*

The Matriarch | G. B. Stern
Introduction by Linda Grant
'Enormously attractive.' – Julia Neuberger

The Invention of Memory | Simon Loftus
'A powerfully evocative mixture of biography and legend.'
– *Financial Times*

Cassandra | Christa Wolf
Translated by Jan Van Heurck
'Filled with passionate and startling insight into human nature.'
– Madeline Miller

2012

A Dance of Folly and Pleasure | O. Henry
'As fresh and alive as the day they were written.' – John Steinbeck

The Architects | Stefan Heym
Afterword by Peter Hutchinson
'Stefan Heym is, by any measure, a literary phenomenon.' – *TLS*

Calm at Sunset, Calm at Dawn | Paul Watkins
'A writer of rare power.' – *Sunday Telegraph*

Illyrian Spring | Ann Bridge
'Reading it is like taking a holiday.' – Kate Kellaway

Life With a Star | Jiří Weil
Translated by Rita Klímová with Roslyn Schloss
'One of the finest novels of the century.' – *Independent*

Kalimantaan | C. S. Godshalk
'A beautifully written, elegant and rich dream.' – John Fowles

2011

American Drolleries | Mark Twain
'Twain is still the liveliest, sharpest most humane
observational satirist and wit.' – A. A. Gill

A Compass Error | Sybille Bedford
'A powerful and merciless book – a classic coming-of-age novel.'
– Hilary Mantel

Mendelssohn is on the Roof | Jiří Weil
Preface by Philip Roth | Translated by Marie Winn
'Comic, sardonic and deeply moving.' – Simon Mawer

A Favourite of the Gods | Sybille Bedford
'One of Britain's most stylish and accomplished writers.'
– *Telegraph*

2010

Improper Stories | Saki
'Heady, delicious and dangerous.' – Stephen Fry